DANCING AROUND THE
VOLCANO

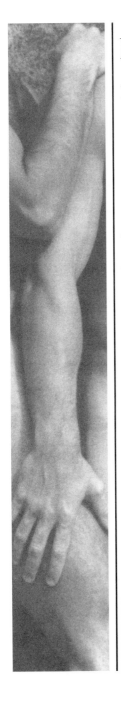

DANCING AROUND THE VOLCANO

FREEING OUR EROTIC LIVES:
DECODING THE ENIGMA OF GAY MEN AND SEX

GUY KETTELHACK

CROWN PUBLISHERS, INC.
NEW YORK

FOR FRANK

Grateful acknowledgment is made to the following for permission to reprint previously published material: Crown Publishers, Inc.: Excerpts from pp. 91, 104–5, and 156–57 from *The Culture of Desire* by Frank Browning. Copyright © 1993 by Frank Browning. Reprinted by permission of Crown Publishers, Inc. Farrar, Straus & Giroux, Inc., and Routledge UK: Excerpt from *Being a Character: Psychoanalysis and Self-Experience* by Christopher Bollas. Copyright © 1992 by Christopher Bollas. Rights in the United Kingdom are adminstered by Routledge UK. Reprinted by permission of Hill and Wang, a division of Farrar, Straus & Giroux, Inc., and Routledge UK. W.W. Norton & Company: Excerpt from *The Many Faces of Eros* by Joyce McDougall. Copyright © 1995 by Joyce McDougall. Reprinted by permission of W.W. Norton & Company. Random House, Inc.: Excerpt from *Sex, Art and American Culture* by Camille Paglia. Copyright © 1992 by Camille Paglia. Reprinted by permission of Vintage Books, a division of Random House, Inc.

Published by Crown Publishers, Inc., 201 East 50th Street, New York, New York 10022. Member of the Crown Publishing Group.

Random House, Inc. New York, Toronto, London, Sydney, Auckland
http://www.randomhouse.com/

CROWN is a trademark of Crown Publishers, Inc.

Printed in the United States of America

Design by Karen Minster

Library of Congress Cataloging-in-Publication Data is available upon request.

ISBN 0-517-70103-0

10 9 8 7 6 5 4 3 2 1

First Edition

CONTENTS

AUTHOR'S NOTE—AND ACKNOWLEDGMENTS

This book is based on material generously shared with me by hundreds of gay men over the past twenty-five years of my life. Because of the intimate nature of their stories, all names and identifying characteristics have been changed to protect anonymity. This adherence to anonymity may seem a bit strange in a book that proclaims the healing rewards of opening up to each other about our sexual lives, feelings, and experiences. However, as open as I believe we need to be about sex, our sexual selves are so subtle and emotionally complex that they deserve, and seem to me to require, an anonymous forum in a book. Any conclusions drawn here are profoundly open-ended, and I do not want to foster the illusion that any man's life can be summed up in a case history with a neat moral. We are more slippery than our momentary pronouncements; fundamental to this book is the idea that as we grow and change, our approaches to sex, love, and relationships change—sometimes radically. The gay men's voices you'll hear in these pages have in this sense been freed by not being tied to, and limited by, the names of "real people."

There is, of course, another, more practical—and sadder—reason for anonymity. We continue to live in a rabidly homophobic society and thus, alas, continue to need to guard the most vulnerable information about ourselves. That said, I've tried to tell a good deal of truth—details, not names—of my own sexual experience. As much as the book seems to me to require keeping other men's stories anonymous, it beckoned to *me* to let 'er rip—and be, if necessary, its sacrificial lamb. Perhaps vainly (in two senses of the word), I hope that my disclosures will beckon to you to tell the truth about your own sexual self; I'd like to think that my example might give some hope that you *can* break the silence and survive—even thrive.

This book is not about AIDS, even though, obviously, no book about sex and gay men can avoid the issue. Sex has for too long been equated with death because of AIDS. We have never more needed a book that separates the two and invites us to explore and once again take joy in the power and mystery of sex, the endless and fascinating information about ourselves we can derive from it. Sex is undoubtedly dangerous—indeed that's a profound premise of this book—but not primarily because of AIDS. As Frank Browning writes in *The Culture of Desire*, "We forget the simplest, plainest truth: To be alive is to be at risk. *Nowhere* can sex be altogether safe, because sex is, for most of us, our primary, residual, atavistic connection to the realm of animal existence." Sex is dangerous because it connects us with the most primal experience of life.

Each man you'll meet in these pages has come to his own peace about the sexual risks he is willing to take. Nothing herein implies or will encourage you to adopt any rigid definition of, or prescriptive advice concerning, "safer sex." My only stance about this topic derives from my most heartfelt aim in these pages, to help you find and cultivate the self in sex, not the self-hate. This inevitably implies an equally heartfelt correlative: do everything you can to live, not die. How you do that is your own business.

I thank the following people for helping me, throughout my life, to understand the multiple journeys this book describes: Donald Thomson, Dennis Gubb, Robert Echols, Peter Johnstone, Bill Cook, D.G., A.F., Luc Gilbert, Ross Jacobs, Hubertus Baumgarten, Chris Mertz, and most especially my war-torn former lover of so many years, Richard Bell, who oversaw so much of my embryonic growth and loved me anyway. Laura Wirth, Orese Fahey, Diana Fanning, Danna Faulds, Robin Harvey, Catherine Synan Green, Ingrid Bartinique, Ann Barker, Marcie Rogers, Dr. Bonnie Jacobson, Donna Boguslav—their friendship and understanding and love have helped me to find the "shaman" aspects of myself that balance out the "warrior." Agent Connie Clausen was my savior when I needed one: when she first met me, in 1982, she saw through the wounded animal and found the writer. My gratitude to her is lifelong. Thanks to Genevieve Field and Elyse Cheney, her assistants, for helping me to hone the proposal that sold this.

Collective thanks to the New York and Boston Centers for Modern Psychoanalytic Studies for helping me to develop the theoretical underpinnings of this book (particularly chapter 4); and particularly to Faye Miller, brilliant analyst and instructor at both centers, for demonstrating that it's possible to bring all of our murderous, yearning, sorrowful, and joyful impulses to consciousness—and survive. Reuven Closter, CSW, the single most important human reason I've been able to translate so many inchoate fears, feelings, longings, and dreams into anything approaching readable prose: he is a magician, a sorcerer, to whom I owe, in some ways, my life as well as the discovery that I had the stuff to write a book like this. A grateful nod to the forces behind the Lesbian, Gay and Bisexual Alliance at my alma mater, Middlebury College, particularly for the forum they gave me in the spring of 1994, where I delivered a sort of proto-version of this book in a talk as part of weekend-long conference on gay, lesbian, and bisexual issues. Immeasurable thanks to Peter Hammond, because he is Huck and I am Tom; Quentin Crisp, the most completely realized human being I know (even if, however unwisely, I have gone ahead and ignored his caveat: "Oh, dear, *don't* tell gay men to have more sex"); David Groff, the editor who acquired this book, who gave me the push off the diving board I needed—and more confidence that I could swim once I hit the water than he knows. Karen Rinaldi, the editor who saw the book through—that outrageously beautiful, brilliant woman who scooped up this book with a passion and an intensity for which I can never adequately thank her—also brought a sharp editorial focus to it, one that has made it a far better book than it would otherwise have been.

It seems a bit disingenuous to express my gratitude to Sigmund Freud, but because I refer to him in these pages, sometimes in ways that may seem unquestioning, a word about his impact on me and this book is in order. I align myself with Jonathan Lear, who (in *Love and Its Place in Nature*) sees Freud as a "speculative metaphysician." The theory and practice of psychoanalysis to which Freud gave birth seems to me more an art than a science, and I find myself stirred, in the same way powerful literature stirs me, by certain principles to which he first gave voice. In other words, I take Freud speculatively, "using" him as a source of some of the most powerful metaphors I've encountered about the birth and development of the human psyche: that's the light in which I hope to have invoked him here.

I'm grateful to have had what amounts to a sound track for the writing of *Dancing Around the Volcano,* the Deutsche Grammophon recording (437 249-2) of Wilhelm Kempff playing the Brahms Fantasies and Intermezzi—the combined artistry and "warrior/shaman" yearning of composer and pianist somehow, mysteriously, added to the form and content of this book (you might, if you like Brahms, put it on as you read). The memory of my brother Robert Alan Kettelhack also permeates every word of this: his message that *joy* is the point of life was and is the light at the end of every tunnel I've faced.

And then there is Frank, to whom this book is dedicated, and to whom I hope to continue to make it clear, for as long as he'll let me, why. I love him with all my fierce and complicated heart.

What perhaps makes sensual pleasure so terrible is that it teaches us we have a body. Up to that point, it has served us only for living. Then we realize that this body has its own special existence, its own dreams, its own will, and that until our death we shall have to take account of it, give in to it, negotiate with it, or struggle against it. We feel (we believe we feel) that our soul is only its finest dream. Sometimes, alone, before a mirror which redoubled my anguish, it would occur to me to ask what I had in common with my body, with its pleasures or its ills, as if I did not belong to it. But I do belong to it, my dear. This body, which appears so fragile, is nonetheless more durable than my virtuous resolutions, perhaps even more durable than my soul.

—Marguerite Yourcenar, *Alexis*

The world exists because we love it.

—Jonathan Lear, *Love and Its Place in Nature*

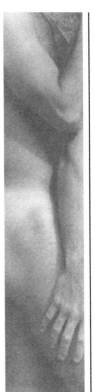

ONE

PAYING ATTENTION TO SEX

I ONCE DESPAIRED OF EVER KNITTING together the Jekyll and Hyde halves of me. Jekyll: the sensitive, caring, responsible, aboveboard public me; Hyde: the dark, sexual, amoral beast. Certainly, for most of my life, Hyde was by far the more fun half, even if the experiences and fantasies he produced have led to (and, in part, been created by) some of my greatest fears, guilts, and conflicts.

A late night I spent about six years ago in a dark S&M cellar in lower Manhattan called the Vault seems to me now a condensation of all that was and is most exciting and satisfying about Hyde. It was after midnight; I was sitting—sprawling back, legs spread wide—in the light of a red lamp on a peeling black vinyl couch, displaying a hairy chest in my open black leather jacket, erasing my eyes with mirror shades (which made the already dim room almost disappear), spotlighting my crotch (the red light hit it squarely on the dick) in a torn, sweaty jockstrap, my feet encased in thick athletic socks and beat-up, black, shit-kicker boots (the rest of my clothes—jeans, basically—had been checked at the door). Ah! What freedom it was to sit back, pat my half-hard cock through the jockstrap pouch, and wait. I felt as if I had all the time in the world: in fact, time had stopped. There was no reality but this dim red darkness, this wonderful eternal expectancy. I was powerful, like a cat in the grass, waiting and watching for prey. If anyone wanted to know who a potent half of the real me was, he had only to take a look at this spotlit, bearded, sweaty man in the corner of the Vault.

A slim piece of prey finally moved in and sat down next to me on the couch; I got a whiff of him from the flannel shirt he was wearing—God, how wonderfully flannel holds a man's scent! He reached over to my jockstrap and stroked my dick through the pouch. I took my shades off and saw a hungry, handsome, young, mustached face. In one strong sweep, I pulled him over with my right hand and kissed him, roughly, deep-throating him. Pliant, sensual, he chewed on my lip a little before I disembarked to lean back for a moment, away from him, to study him, look in his eyes, which seemed both to beseech and challenge. He produced that involuntary curl of the lip that all men seem to produce when they dunk a basketball, dance, fuck, or get fucked: a hormonal male challenge, a concentrated look of male aggression. Suddenly, almost absently, I backhand slapped him, lightly, in the face, to see how he'd respond to rougher treatment. He moaned softly, *"Ah, oui, oui . . . Encore . . ."*

Good God: he was French. He spoke almost no English. This made him perfect—European, foreign, an ideal dreamlike man to play with on this couch in this cellar, no need to talk, only to touch—disembodied, almost; no reality past the smell and heft of him in my arms, past the feeling of his hand stroking my dick, past the fantasy in which he was a willing participant, past the sheer complete feeling of animality, of maleness, that suffused me and made me feel alive.

This felt like the secret, truest me—the part I kept hidden from the bright public world in which I felt forced to spend my daylight hours. I could only be myself in the dark. And I was convinced that the components of me I called Jekyll—the aspiring psychoanalyst, the talented violinist, the writer who spoke warmly to civilized editors and colleagues—were, while true enough effusions of my personality, still mainly the surface of me. They didn't get to the heart—or the balls. Satisfying Jekyll's needs didn't have anywhere near the impact and relief of satisfying Hyde's.

However, the meaning of this moment—of allowing Hyde full play—didn't really deepen until the following morning. I had a planning session with one of the psychologists with whom I was collaborating on a book, one in a series of "how to be happy" self-help books directed mainly to heterosexual women, which had lately become my largest stock-in-trade. As I sat with my ebullient coauthor, a woman who had a thriving (almost entirely heterosexual) practice, and whom I respected and liked for what seemed to be her unshakable and contagious optimism about the human capacity for positive change, my mind kept darting back to the previous night in the Vault. The sun poured into her office; the psychologist was talking about a shy, mousy woman who did not believe her opinion counted for anything, who was accommodating to a devastating fault, but who, in group session, finally took a leap—for the first time in her therapeutic life, she disagreed, at first quietly, and then with greater passion, with someone else in the group. As she drummed up her courage to express a passionate opinion, it was as if she had lit some inner fire: her eyes blazed, she came to unprecedented life. The group was silent as she gained momentum; they had never seen her emerge so strongly, so singularly, so vividly, before. I forget what it was she was disagreeing about; but the content of her thought wasn't the point. Her passion was the point. Her emergence was the point.

As I listened, I relived the excitement I had felt in the Vault, the anticipation of some primal contact, the audacity of showing my sexual self so blatantly, and realized that the freedom I felt was not so different from my coauthor's description of this mouse-turned-lioness. Some column of fire was allowed to burst forth; some pure current of *self* forged its way through the woman's wary defenses, and she was transformed. My Vault moment was pivotal not because it was new—I had found numerous dark ways to let this sexual beast out before—but because, now, the morning after, in this sunny psychologist's office, it *meshed* with my daylight world. It did not seem so irrevocably *apart*. Managing appetites, managing the psyche's ache to express itself (battling powerful defenses against self-expression), was something that drove me, drove the mouse/lioness, continually—in the light as well as the dark. My mind freely darted back to other images in the Vault, other men there in the red sexual dimness, six or so males clustering in the corner watching two godlike twenty-one-year-olds kiss and slowly disrobe each other; the frightened men, the men who watched nervously from the sidelines, the men who kept their clothes on, eyes wide, unsure of what it was they wanted, or that they had the right and the wherewithal to get it. I saw a spectrum of selves wrestling with their ids, alternately resisting and giving in to the force of their columns of fire. I felt my own "sadistic" sexual urges again, the satisfaction of getting rough with my Frenchman, his willing receptivity to my fire; somehow in the light of the psychologist's office, in the light of my day-life, it was suddenly clear to me how volcanic this psychic urge to "be" is—how it never lets up, despite the formidable resistances we set against it. My psychologist's lioness, this formerly locked-up heterosexual woman, suddenly lit from within, crept into the Vault with me and looked around and smiled. "Yes," she seemed to say in this vision, "I see what you're doing. Go for it."

Go for what? What were all these consenting gay male adults consenting *to?* Simply to use each other in "forbidden" sexual ways: to "act out" aggressions in the most direct manner possible? No—the consent went deeper and wider than that. The consent was *internal* before it was external: each of these men responded to an inner call from the ego to the id: "Come out, Hyde, I need you." The Red Sea of the vast and imperious superego (the conscience) parted, and a huge dark, muscular army of sex was allowed to plow through. The consent was, even if consigned for many of these men entirely to the 2 A.M. darkness of the Vault (and to no other conscious part of their lives), between and among the warring parts of each of these men's selves.

That "Red Sea" is formidable for most gay men: when it rushes back to drown the army (which it almost always does after the army fucks itself to completion, or—as in the case of the wary wallflowers in the Vault—sorrowfully admits defeat), it can rush in with a terrible vengeance. "How *dare* you summon up this army? You're sick. You're evil. You're an unspeakable animal. Go home and repent." The sources of this Red Sea are deep and lifelong, but they are not only the external forces of family and culture holding (still holding) the very idea of homosexuality in vicious contempt. The warring elements in us are *internal,* too. They are part of the bargain of being human. The *war,* in other words, is inescapable, and societal change—making homosexuality more culturally acceptable—will not entirely solve the conflict. The catch-22 is that we *need* our superegos: they give us necessary boundaries; they may keep us from killing ourselves. Most exasperatingly, they give form to our fantasies; their proscriptions fuel a good deal of what makes sexual fantasy "hot" (taboo). The superego is not the enemy; neither is the eternally starving id. The ego—the conscious sense of self—must mediate between these two powerful forces, one eruptive, the other repressive, in an almost continual state of tension. When one force overcomes the other, balance must be restored for the ego to go on functioning in the daylight world. Achieving this balance is a bitch; but there's no way out of the conflict. Jekyll may indeed learn to acknowledge Hyde's existence, first grudgingly, then with some kind of acceptance, even for moments, love— but they're going to get into a brawl before any such "acceptance" can be even momentarily achieved.

This capsule of my version of Jekyll and Hyde (and its aftermath) invariably produces some measure of identification in every gay man I have met. I don't mean that every gay man I have met is into S&M, has acted out the "darker" Hyde elements of his personality, likes anonymous sex, or is even in as much conflict as I have been over the split-off sexual self and the self who talks to his mother and boss. But I have never met a gay man who does not have a sharp and profound sense of what it means to have an "outer" and an "inner" self—especially with regard to sex. The problem is, we've been encouraged to believe this war is abnormal, a sign of sickness; we've been encouraged to believe in, even to aspire to achieve, what I hold to be an entirely false model of "integrated" self: if only we'd be good boys, if only we'd learn to behave in the dark, we'd be happy and conflict free.

Don't count on it.

Not that this is saying anything particularly new or remarkable: what human being doesn't experience some version of this division between good chaste child and bad sexual kid? But gay men have gone to such extraordinary, imaginative lengths to adapt to their divisions, even while we may also go to extraordinary lengths to cover up our adaptations. No one has, to my satisfaction, reported on the lessons of managing Jekyll and Hyde and the other archetypes who grapple for power in the gay male psyche. We are typically fearful and/or defensive in this realm of Hieronymus Bosch: but while our behavioral poles may range from the defiant L.A. S&M leatherman "proud" of his difference from the norm to the boy from Ohio who wants to settle down with a spouse and bring up a dog or even a child, the sources and details of their inner landscapes of dreams and fantasies may link the L.A. top and the Ohio kid more closely and in more unusual ways than either of them supposes.

This book will explore that link.

I would like to tell another story about myself, more difficult and painful to reveal than the dreamlike "condensation" of Hyde with which I roped you into this chapter. I would like to tell you how I learned to pay attention to sex—how I learned what, with the help of scores of other gay men's voices and experiences, I would like to pass on to the L.A. top and the Ohio kid and you.

But before I talk about the pain, let me talk about the triumph, in more detail than I offered in the foregoing overview.

RECLAIMING THE BEAST

As outrageous (and, possibly, distasteful or even pathetic) as that half-naked me in the Vault may strike you, my ability to be there and feel what I was feeling marked a good deal of progress for me. Sprawled exhibitionistically on that couch, provocatively dressed, without the aid of drugs or alcohol, simply enjoying being a sexual beast, I had attained a level of self-love—call it narcissism—that was unprecedented for a boy who once wasn't entirely sure he existed. Before this, I had only been able to claim the sexual beast in me by getting plowed: alcohol was my royal road to the unconscious, a superego solvent that momentarily ripped away the self-hating, internalized parental and societal voices that told me, endlessly, how and in what ways I was pitifully lacking. Before that, I had felt, like so many other gay boys growing up in a society that holds them in contempt, visible only when I could, by some force of imaginative will, pretend to be someone "acceptable."

I think what strikes me most about this memory of the Vault is how *physical* I felt: what a huge contrast, once again, to the boy who hadn't felt any real connection to his own body, probably since infancy (when I take it on faith I did have some bodily sense of myself). Even when I managed—with the aid of alcohol and drugs—to pursue and sometimes experience physical, sexual pleasure, it was a very tentative contact with "the beast" at best. A painful self-consciousness was never far off; when anyone rejected me (in a bar, at the baths, in the woods of Fire Island), my self-hate came flooding back. Certainly, sober, I would never have allowed myself to expose my less-than-Apollonian body as I did later on in the Vault. I drank, in the days that I drank, to erase my terrible certainty that I was under- and overendowed exactly where I ought to have been the reverse. So, joying in my "beast-ness" meant I had come a long way. I sometimes think I've picked up where I left off at some unremembered moment in childhood before my superego clamped down: sometimes, with my lover today, I'll sit naked, cross-legged, and look down at my hairy male body in wonder—joying in my physicality—loving the sweat, the balls, the dick, the now middle-aged body I had once found literally unspeakable.

We grow up unpredictably; my mistake was in thinking that

this physical acceptance I'd achieved after so many years was the end of growth. In fact, it was only the barest beginning.

When I first conceived of this book, I thought of it mainly as a paean to gay male sexuality—to our erotic inventiveness, to the uses to which we put sex (recreation, a way to meet each other, a way to explore the darker, more mysterious realms of ourselves, as well as a way to "make love"), to the enormous variety of relationships we construct to satisfy this imperious urge. It seemed to me urgent for us to learn to rejoice in our imaginative experience of sex, to talk to each other about it, accept the endless accommodations we make to it, especially in the backlash age of AIDS where sex, for too many people, is equated with death. It seemed to me just as urgent to accept that *conflict* was always going to be part of sex; that we were naive to think we could banish it. Sex, in other words, is always a "problem"; it's always going to goad us, taunt us, beckon to us. "There is," Quentin Crisp advises us, "no great dark man": no perfect partner or sublime experience that will put an end, forever, to the disturbance, confusion, and urgency that are part of the flesh of sex, the stuff of being human. My European friends seemed (condescendingly) bemused by the American gay male obsession with The Perfect Body, as if that could possibly be an easy answer to sex—or even invariably erotic. Our fiercely Puritan reaction to the sins of Clarence Thomas, Heidi Fleiss, Hugh Grant: these all seemed to be sordid but hardly rare—indeed, nearly ubiquitous—foibles of being human to everyone but Americans. Puritanism isn't all that plagues us: we are psychic imperialists, still burdened by a nineteenth-century idea of progress—that a morally homogeneous "utopia" is not only achievable, but it is our manifest destiny to achieve it (by next Tuesday).

In fact, life is chaotic. Things rarely happen on cue, or as planned—especially not feelings, and certainly not sex. But while there may be no "great dark man," there can be wonderful "great dark moments." And I wanted this book to explore them, to report on the lessons these moments have taught us. This is not, in any conventional sense, a book about relationships or love. It is meant to be a book about self-discovery. Love, if it happened, would happen on its own. I knew the voices of gay men I was collecting would tell us about love—but these revelations would come through the back door, indirectly. *Sex* was the mystery I wanted to plumb in this book, and I believed it could be somehow independently sorted out from other emotional, psychic, and physical phenomena—that by paying attention to our sexual behavior, we could learn what it was we were really after.

Books bare the souls of their writers. I wanted to explore the "uses" of sex because I was having such a remarkable time finding out the uses of sex in my own life. I felt like a pioneer: at the age of forty, I extracted myself from a twelve-and-a-half-year relationship with a man I truly did love, but from whom I felt I had irretrievably grown apart, not least sexually. It was a part of my delayed growth to leave that relationship and create a home for myself: I had never received a utilities bill before; it had always been in somebody else's name. I yearned so terribly for "independence": a real, rooted—and for me unprecedented—sense of autonomy. And I yearned for an *open* sexual smorgasbord: to leave outrageous sexual messages on telephone lines, to be open about the fact that I was meeting as many men as I wanted to meet, to strut my stuff—to go to places like the Vault and not lie about them. I'd been to places like that before, of course, but *had* lied about them: to everyone in the Jekyll part of my life. This included my ex-lover; as it had lovers before him.

There was an absolute split, to me, between having a lover and having an uninhibited sexual life. It was a split I didn't consciously set out to heal, setting my home up in my little Christopher Street studio: in fact, I was more conscious of wanting to give in to Hyde—do his bidding. *Safely* enough: I had stopped drinking seven years before I moved into my home; I was no longer on the self-destructive path I'd once been on. My brother had died of AIDS; the plague was very real to me and I had no conscious desire to kill myself with wanton unprotected sex. But I did want to have fun. More than that: I wanted to live the adventure I knew my life could be. I had a number of books under contract, which meant enough money to comb flea markets and construct the Edwardian bordello I'd already been living in, for years, in my imagination. It came together as easily as dominoes fall: framed Victorian photographs, quantities of pillows, burgundy drapes and swags of cheap East Village satin ropes, with boxing gloves tacked over my bed and a huge photograph of Judy Garland in the bathroom and framed ads of 1959 General Motors cars (giving loud expression to three formerly secret obsessions) adding an even quirkier twist—I let out my id all over the walls.

I wrote and had sex and ate buttered noodles and racked up too much debt on credit cards—sending me to London more times than I could really afford to go. In other words, I picked up on my babyhood, going back to that aforementioned unremembered moment when I somehow learned I couldn't be who I was. I was damned if I wasn't going to be who I was this time around. I felt I had a whole life to make up for.

The sexual explorations I made were as outrageous, sometimes, as my apartment. At the age of forty-one, balancing sex-friendships with about four men, to each of whom I was careful to say I was *not* looking for a monogamous lover (the honesty was exhilarating!), I went about having my hedonistic good time. During this period of exploration the idea for this book emerged: I was amazed, first of all, at the unstoppable sexual energy of gay men in New York. No matter that places like the Mineshaft and the Anvil had long been shut down: gay male libido had created dozens of new venues for sex—popping up like mushrooms all over the city. AIDS has, in some cases, changed our sexual behavior, but it hasn't changed our volcanic sexual energy one whit. I had always been tempted to see this out-and-out endless orgy (at least as portrayed by New York's weekly sex mags, *HX* and *Next*) as some sort of pathology: in other words, I'd bought into the widely held heterosexual disapproval—resentment—of all these kids *playing* all the time. And that's what I suppose I was learning to do: play. For longer and longer moments, all anxiety fell out of me, off me, lightening me. There didn't seem anything I couldn't do, couldn't have, couldn't be.

I often think of the island all those little boys were spirited off to in Disney's *Pinocchio*: an island encouraging the kids to go over the top with self-indulgent *play,* with as many sweets and rides and little-boy amusements as you could cram into your day. Disney, as unforgiving a moralist as John Bunyan *(Pinocchio* has always seemed to me to be his cartoon version of *Pilgrim's Progress),* makes these naughty boys grow donkey ears. I didn't grow donkey ears, but I did discover that something else was going on besides play.

The *people* you played with: that was the problem. That had always been the problem before, too. Any lover I'd had in the past had quickly lost some essential "maleness" I was hungry for. Perhaps I killed it off myself: I couldn't, as I've said, square the Hyde of raw male-animal sex with the Jekyll of monogamous marriage. One had to go. I didn't know how to be with someone without chopping off the maleness: it couldn't survive the superego-driven "love." But even in my smorgasbord of sexual fun, where I was careful to hold the reins back and not become a monogamous husband to anyone, I nonetheless kept barging into even my casual sex-buddies' emotional—*human*—individuality. As much as I wanted to keep them as satisfying (essentially featureless and functional) as my Frenchman in the Vault, their emotional idiosyncracies, this peculiar selfness, kept rocking me. I realized, with every awkward bump into my sex partners' idiosyncratic reality, that I was missing something in this great feast of a smorgasbord—something I couldn't find on the menu, vast as it was. Something deeper wasn't being touched. I don't even mean I missed "love"—although that might be one word I'd use for it now. I missed going deeper. I missed the fear and thrill and adventure and mystery of allowing myself to enter somebody else's life.

FROM BEAST TO LOVER

The urge to connect more deeply with another man set up the dominoes that ended in meeting the lover I'm with today. I met him in the usual way—usual to my smorgasbord days: I'd left a hot S&M message on the Dungeon Line (it's amazing how easy it is to fall into the supermale gym-teacher voice that so frightened me back in junior high; I was a big, sadistic, sweaty top looking for a passive kid who could "take it"— whatever we wanted "it" to be). My lover was one of the men who answered it. It's hard to bring back the first reality of him— I was so determined to keep him a player in our little scene, and as I've said, I was expressly *not* looking for a lover. I remember him, first, as sweet, pliant, excited—obviously tuned into my own sexual wavelength—but I wanted him to be a toy, so I treated him like a toy. Our first encounter was hot (involving creative use of handcuffs and inspired verbal fantasy); he was a kid to me— an adventurer. It impressed me that he was willing to act out his fantasies, not just have them in his head. He was a kid who took risks. And he was smart. That's what hooked me, I think: I couldn't keep him only a piece of kid-meat for long. A lightning-quick mind was in this "boy" (thirty-one when I met him): a curiosity and receptivity and critical acumen darting about those big brown Greek eyes. We did something after our first sex date I hadn't done before: we went out for coffee at a nearby café. Something in those eyes hooked me, spoke to the capacity I'd inadvertently developed for deeper feeling. But I kept it only a flicker: all I knew was that I wanted to see him again.

So I did. The sex continued to be hot; but the talk warmed up, too. He had a kind of abrupt, leaping, intuitive mind, very different from the rambling Jamesian circuits into which my own more literary intelligence drags me. He was bracing—exciting, impatient, a kind of brilliant child, full of energy, ready to express whatever feeling or thought flitted through his head, Mediterranean, blinding sun alternating with great dark, quick passing clouds—and unbelievably sexual. I was experiencing him more hungrily and completely and deeply than I meant to. Again, a deeper emotional road in me had been plowed: something in my psyche had already unconsciously decided it wanted something essential in this man. Consciously, it took me much longer to catch up and realize it.

I realized it when he came to an orchestra concert I was in—I was playing a florid violin solo in a Corelli concerto grosso. The Upper West Side church was gratifyingly packed; I played as well as I've ever played. I didn't see him until after it was over. In fact, I didn't see him, at first, even when I was looking right at him. When I did finally see him, recognize him, let his reality into my compartmentalized mind, a little explosion went off. He was dressed up in jacket and tie. He looked stunningly handsome. In a flash, I felt a terrible wrench in my gut: I have no other words for it than to say that I knew I was in love. We walked to his car after the concert so he could drive me downtown; I fumbled into the wrong side of the car. I felt like a sixteen-year-old.

I kept darting glances at him: what had changed? Why was I now so suddenly receptive to something against which I had for so long, so carefully, defiantly guarded myself? What was this feeling? Why was it so strong?

The furrows plowed by my desire for connection now heartily drank in the rain of him, the seed of him, the promise of some unprecedented crop. In the following months, we tip-toed around the sides of the pool, cajoling each other with encouraging words, and finally, each of us dived in: by January 1, 1993, we decided we were "lovers."

Lovers—oh, God, I certainly dreaded that word. But I was convinced it was different this time—and in many ways it was. For one thing, I didn't leap to make plans to live with him. A lover had always meant to me that you instantly grafted onto each other, mixed your belongings, and settled into the same physical (if not always psychic) room. My little Edwardian bordello was still too precious to me to give up: this symbol and sense of autonomous self had been dearly bought and wasn't something I was prepared to give up easily. He, too, didn't feel the need or desire to "merge" as completely as all that. I was thrilled he wasn't overbearingly needy, the way so many men I'd been involved with in the past seemed to be. D. H. Lawrence's ideal of two eagles meeting and mating in the sky: that was the independent union he and I would have. Certainly we fantasized about sharing a home: an inspired architect, he pored over the real estate section of the Sunday *New York Times* in search of the perfect dilapidated, sprawling three-bedroom that he could transform into a glorious spread, my den on one end, his on the other.

The sex continued to be incredible—which was incredible to me. Calling him a lover did not, as it always had before, drain the maleness out of him or me. I realize now I had never met a lover fantasy-first before. A peculiar dividend of meeting on sex phone lines is that the men you talk to know some of the most basic and intimate information about you *first:* this man and I knew we were already on a good deal of the same sexual wavelength. But more than that, we beckoned to the most creative sexual parts of ourselves. We are both risk-takers. We wanted to see how much excessive pleasure we could pile on—how far we could take our fantasies. Sometimes it threatened to get out of hand: did he *really* want to get that brutally worked over? (Did I really want to do it to him?) I discovered—as he did—new realms of what I have come to think of as my Warrior self; we took ourselves to the brink of any number of precipices and caught ourselves just before falling off. We discovered, together, the *danger* of sex. We got closer than either of us ever had to its double-edged power—the power to destroy, even to kill, was a hairbreadth away from the power to attract and connect. We danced around the *rim* of the volcano.

But we also shared immense tenderness. One early persistent pattern asserted itself: after coming, we would lie in bed, he would nestle under my right arm and start softly to drift off, snore, clutching to me like an infant, while I'd breathe softly and deeply and look out the window of my little room—what wonderful nineteenth-century fancies I had, listening to Mahler (the *Kindertotenlieder!*) as my baby slept softly on my chest. I had felt no greater bliss.

But we also discovered our differences. Some of these split predictably: my lover has southern European roots, I am northern; he expresses; I withdraw. Sexually, he has intense fantasies about "Guido" sharp dressers, Mafia peacock types in perfect thin Italian shoes, sheer socks, carefully tailored but showy double-breasted suits, scrubbed clean, smelling of cologne, hair slicked back, tough but smooth. I was the me who stripped down, sweated, and smelled in the Vault: an earthy, blunt beast. As usual, our fantasies were at great removes from the public Jekyll selves we showed most of the world. He had gone to Ivy League schools and was perfectly well behaved, charming, funny, in public; I was what he called a "sweetheart": full of empathy and compassion, not an aggressive bone in my (public) body. We each had profound childhood reasons for latching onto our alter-Hyde selves, reasons we began to think about and explore with each other—as long as they didn't take away from the slick-Guido and earthy-beast fantasies they'd fueled, which we did *not* want to give up.

I was discovering realms of sex I had never explored with someone I loved: I let out a sharp and deep sigh of relief. Hyde had met Jekyll! My split had healed! The two halves of me could coexist—and dance around the volcano with each other!

But it wasn't so simple.

FROM LOVER TO HUMAN BEING

As much as I thought of him as a lover, he was still a playmate I kept in a compartment—a large compartment, but held away from the rest of my life. I know now that I didn't truly believe I could share all of who I was with him. The split in me wasn't just between Jekyll and Hyde. There was the psychoanalytic me; the me who only felt alive in 1895 London; the rambling Jamesian me; and the sexual-receptive me who was quite different from the Warrior top I had presented so floridly and completely to him. As the months went on, as we grew to accept our weekend relationship (he lives and works in Queens, which sucked up his daily life, and allowed me to continue my private world on Christopher Street), we fell, I now see, into patterns that deepened and had their satisfactions but kept all of who we were apart from each other.

Another significant continuity: we both still loved listening to the messages on phone lines. The problem: he could listen and satisfy himself with fantasy, sometimes calling a particularly erotic message leaver but never meeting him; it was too easy and too tempting for me to go that further step. The volcano of sex would not stop erupting—and I could not entirely channel its power into the "lover" relationship we had together. It was too ingrained in me to grab for what I wanted in the dark, to deny myself nothing, to keep myself on the old track of sneaking my way to sexual pleasure. There was a split now between whom I thought I had to be with my lover, and who I was privately, in my own little world. I did not know—did not, I think, believe—that I could share more of myself than I was already sharing with him. And so, at periods of anxiety when it seemed as if nothing but the old raw anonymous contact could satisfy, I'd connect physically with this or that messenger: the phone lines still produced a few anonymous male bodies for me, bodies I met with in secret, sexual outlets I convinced myself did not alter the rest of my life. It's what I had always done, always turned to before. I could think of no other recourse to feed the fires that sometimes flared up in me so unbearably.

Fidelity: are gay men incapable of it? That's what I thought, finally, even though I tried to convince myself otherwise—pleading with my lover to understand that I did want a monogamous relationship with him even as I continued secretly to have my isolated peccadilloes. When this had happened before—and it happened a great deal in my last relationship, to the point where my ex-lover was convinced I was a sociopath, so fervently did I lie about not having extracurricular sex—it became just more fuel to add to my always simmering self-hate. Maybe I *was* a sociopath; maybe I just wasn't capable of the kind of "intimacy" that "mature" people were able to find in marriage. Hadn't I always felt like damaged goods, as if something essential were missing in me?

How could I stop satisfying my urgent hunger for contact in the only way I'd been able to find to satisfy it?

But while I resumed my old duplicity with my current lover, something in me wasn't buying that I had to continue this split. For one thing, my dissatisfaction with the compartments into which I'd placed the two of us was provoking more than the odd extracurricular anonymous sexual encounter. I truly *wanted* to connect with him more widely, deeply, completely. I did, after all, want to be more completely seen by him. I began to insist that he read my writing—something I'd previously decided really didn't interest him. Part of the limits of the compartment I'd constructed were he was visual, I was verbal. I showed him home movies of my childhood. I talked about the excitement I had in the courses in psychoanalysis I was taking. I played music for him, trying to get him to understand what it was about the Brahms First Symphony, Mozart's *Symphonie Konzertante,* the young Judy Garland's voice, that so riveted me. I suppose I began to storm against the walls I myself had constructed to confine us.

And he came through for me. I *could* after all talk to him. He read my first novel and actually cried from its impact: he was astonishingly insightful about it, astonishing to me who had thought him uninterested in the parts of me that weren't sexual "top." There was more to him than I had allowed myself to see. He shared his own dreams and aspirations about being an artist and architect. His talents, mind, and soul were as limitless as he found my own. We were still often exasperating; he was still often a cranky child who drove me crazy; my passive-aggressive instinct was to shut down. But slowly, perhaps because we tired of keeping so much pent up and away from each other, we began to break our usual cycle. We started listening to each other without exploding or bolting away.

Slowly the urge in me to connect anonymously began a

sea change: it began to fade. I remember wanting to tell him about these past extracurricular forays, but he'd made it clear he was a vengeful Greek and would never forgive my "cheating on" him. The 1950s B-movie phrase made my heart sink: I despaired of his ever understanding this confusing, urgent part of me. Didn't he realize that it was always more complicated than "cheating on"?

But in fact I had cheated him. I had lied to him, not just about the sexual encounters I'd had in secret, but about what I needed, what my fears and urges and thoughts really were—who I was. *Cheating* was the right word. I know now that he sensed I was having outside sex; some radar made him zero in on a phone message he realized would turn me on; he phoned the man and discovered that he had had sex with me. In a dreadful, cold, even, furious voice, he called me and demanded that I tell him "the truth." So I did.

The truth was: I had withheld much of who I was from him. I had not truly realized, accepted, that he was a full feeling human being whom I could hurt. I did not realize that my actions toward him truly had consequences. Somehow, essentially, I had kept him a version of the Frenchman at the Vault—someone who existed only to play a limited role in my life, someone I could only let in under limited and guarded conditions. It was frightening to admit these things. It meant facing my own defensive, secret, scurrying self head-on. It meant I had to make a choice.

That I am making that choice—to be all of who I am with my lover, to channel these volcanic energies in his direction, and to accept his own eruptions (no easy task, God knows)—is astonishing to me because self-hate is, finally, not a motive for making it. I have certainly not banished conflict in making this choice—the ways I've compartmentalized lust and love (to name only two compartments) have an entrenched, lifelong strength and force. There are still times when I don't feel equal to the task of giving that divided self up. But when I return to the *feeling*—the life-affirming, joyous feeling of connecting in deeper ways with my lover, the feeling that impels me to explore monogamy with my lover—once again the selves in me find compelling purpose to coalesce. Not that the achievement of monogamy is necessarily the greatest good; I have no illusions about how severe the internal battles can be in two men attempting to be sexually faithful to each other. It is an adventure I very much want to explore, but it's not for everyone, nor should it be. I see, as the warring selves in me begin to integrate, that every moment and every experience I've undergone, including my ambivalent infidelities, had their important lessons. I cherish all of those moments; I judge none of them, except to note, when I can, what role each experience seems to have had in bringing me to the bend of the road I'm now pursuing.

Every moment of my sexual life and experience illuminates the hunger of other gay men who have felt what I have felt and allows me to accept, and have compassion for, what they may think of as their most shameful, inadmissible sexual excesses. I know now there is much to be found in those excesses, but that you can't find it by damning yourself. You learn from your sexual behavior by giving yourself permission to explore it, be curious, accept it, think and talk about it, respect what it's giving you, even enjoy it. In that mode of self-acceptance, you're in a better position to choose the direction you want your adventure to take. Sexual monogamy is one of many journeys; this book will explore many disparate gay men whose routes to sexual self-honesty and pleasure are very different from mine—there are countless ways to integrate. Choices range from a joyous promiscuity to marriage-with-dog-and-kids. Hustlers sometimes lead satisfying lives; so do celibate monks.

Do not expect this movement toward integration to be easy

or predictable: we are, after all, dealing with a volcano here. But don't shy away from whatever truth you discover about yourself as you climb toward or away from that volcano's rim. Gay men have *used* sex so ingeniously; that's what I mean to celebrate and explore in this book. I think you will learn from the uses and rewards of sex you'll find in these pages that there's more in sexual fantasy and reality than you realized—more richness, mystery, adventure, and so much more information about who you are and what you want.

This book is, however, more than a celebration of gay male sexuality. It also attempts to address—and in some mysterious way even embrace—conflict, ambivalence, the full tangled reality of what it means not only to be sexual, but to be human. The broad areas we'll be exploring—some of the uses of sex that may not be so obvious, attempting to acknowledge and understand more about the archetypal drives that create each of our unique takes on sex, questioning some assumptions about pathology that hold as much sway in the 1990s as they did in the 1950s, and finally exploring what it means for the psyche to integrate its warring fears and drives not only in sex but in life—all of this constitutes an invitation. I want to invite you to look at your own warring internal sexual universe, as much of it as you can make conscious, without instantly judging it, rationalizing it, or hating it. Hating the Jekyll or the Hyde or the Warrior or the Shaman or the Tom of Finland or the RuPaul singing and fucking and fighting and cowering inside you is cruelly pointless. Each of these selves yearns to tell you something important: they each deserve the most curious and compassionate attention you can give them.

I now know that Jekyll is no less a part of me than Hyde: I was wrong about the Vault self being the "truest." Every part of me—every part of you—is true. If this book helps to bring you one step closer to allowing your own selves to coexist, I will consider it a leaping success.

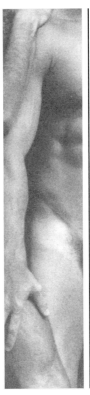

TWO

THE
USES
OF
SEX

I LOVE <u>STEAM</u> MAGAZINE: IT'S A RE-
freshing, collective howl of lust. Its purpose—"a quarterly magazine intended for gay and bisexual men with an interest in public
and semi-public sex . . . to provide a sex-positive forum for sub-
jects considered 'taboo' by other mags"—doesn't quite prepare
the uninitiated for the range of "taboo" sex it celebrates. A random sampling of articles from the autumn 1994 issue: "Looking
for Sex in Croatia and Slovenia," "The Sleazehound Hall of
Fame," "Chicago—Shoulders Ain't All That's Big," "My Favorite Gloryhole."

There is, to me, something exhilarating about the un-
abashed celebration of sex in *Steam,* wherever it can be found,
in the bushes of parks, abandoned buildings of wharves, men's
rooms of bus stations, or even Croatia and Slovenia. But I think

what most astonishes me is its revolutionary message, which is also the explicit and/or implicit message of such magazines as *Drummer*, the late Boyd McDonald's wonderful laconic *Straight to Hell* reports of "true sex adventures," New York's gay-sex guides *Next* and *HX*. The message is one most gay men have swallowed without blinking: *we deserve as much sex as we want with whomever we can get to have it with us*. What a proposition to accept so calmly! This universe of sex invites us, simply and directly, to take as much of what it offers as we can handle, and that's a bargain few of us, at least when we're horny, have ever turned down, much less questioned.

Steam may be a little over-the-top for some gay men (who frown on the rampant "public" sex the magazine howls about), but *HX* and *Next* magazines can be found on the coffee table of even the most conservative gay man in New York, offering weekly orgasmic opportunities that would make his heterosexual counterpart's jaw drop. A random alphabetical sampling: Afro-diziak ("private safe-sex party for African-American men every Friday night"), Attic Antics ("Que sera sera. General sleaze party every 2nd and 4th Thursday"), Blow Buddies ("Down and direct oral action"), Carter's NY Prime ("for well-built men interested in private parties"), The Hangman's Club ("open only to men with 8+ inch equipment"), and on through the alphabet to Zone DK ("Dungeon playground"). This vast sexual circus is full of men, every night of every week, in New York. It partly defines what it *means* to be gay in New York. Chicago, San Francisco, Los Angeles, Dallas, Houston, Miami, Montreal—all have their equivalents. Gay men are *out* there (dammit) and we're getting (or endlessly fantasizing about getting) our rocks off.

The feast we provide ourselves is in many ways quite wonderful. Our prodigious sexual imaginations and behavior tell us we know what we want and that we're devising endless exciting ways of getting it. But I find it fascinating that we participate in this feast to whatever degree we do (Blow Buddies, from all accounts, is packed every Tuesday night) without ever really acknowledging it. As loud as the sexual advertisements are, as completely as we succumb to their promises, we're silent about it.

Why? Some familiar reasons suggest themselves: we're secretly ashamed of these sexual blasts; our internalized homophobia tells us that all this sex is pathological; we still feel somehow bad or different or sick for being so sexually fixated. In short, while this abundance of sex might be fun, it's finally immoral. We partake of it on the sly, in the dark, in silence, because it's wrong. The bargain of Blow Buddies and Afro-diziak is a false one. All this sex is really only empty, narcissistic, dehumanizing—not to say physically dangerous. There's no love in it. It's not mature. And we're certainly not being morally responsible when we give in to it.

A NEW LOOK AT
MORAL RESPONSIBILITY

As old-fashioned as some of the above reasons may seem to be, they are bred into us by culture and family with enormous strength. And they may sound, even now—some of them may even *be*—completely plausible. Even, by your system of beliefs, right.

But the way we determine whether or not our behavior (sexual or otherwise) is right seems to me to need examination.

We seem to approach moral responsibility in two ways. One (and by my observation the most common) is to measure how we behave against what we believe. What we believe is the standard; how we behave is a measure of how steadfastly we adhere to the standard. Thus, the gay man with a lover who professes to believe in monogamy but nonetheless regularly finds himself on his knees in the local gay movie house servicing various anonymous men will, by this way of measuring moral responsibility, find himself woefully lacking.

The second way of approaching moral responsibility is to reverse the equation: to look at how we behave first and measure what we say we believe against that behavior. This approach means not only looking at what we are doing, but accepting that we are doing it: accepting the *fact* of the behavior before we assign a belief to it. The man on his knees in the movie house might, taking this approach, learn from his behavior that he doesn't after all believe in sexual monogamy and that, in his scheme of things, anonymous sex is exciting and rewarding and something he doesn't want to give up. He will have located his true belief by taking a close look at how he behaves.

He might, of course, come up with any number of other conclusions. His feelings about what he's doing are clues just as important about the belief underlying them as the behavior itself; he may discover, by attending to these feelings, that he doesn't actually believe either in monogamy *or* the sort of anonymous sex he's now having; he may only have discovered that he's hungry for *something*—contact, attention, affection—that he's blindly seeking to sate. At this stage, the clearest definition of a belief may simply be "I believe I'm empty—and that I must do anything I can to be filled."

The point is that whatever we may say we believe, our actions give the lie—or perhaps the real truth—to it: they are the more accurate measure of what we really believe. The men I have listened to, the men whose stories fill this book, have all to large degrees taken this behavioral approach to morals: tried to examine the evidence of their behavior, and their feelings about that behavior, for the beliefs that evidence implies.

This doesn't mean that every man I've talked to has been

ecstatic about his findings. An HIV-positive man who fucks another man without a condom may look at his behavior and discover that his real belief runs something like this: "I hate everyone who doesn't have AIDS and I want everyone to die just like I'm going to. So I'm going to give my disease to everyone I can." Once he's located the rage and hate in this belief, once he's articulated to himself what his behavior is really telling him he believes, he may well decide that he is more ambivalent about this belief than he knew and that, on closer reflection, he might give more effective vent to his rage and hate by expressing it verbally more directly—and less dangerously—to the rest of the world.

Reconciling behavior to belief, managing the Jekyll and Hyde aspects of ourselves, is not necessarily easier when we take the behavior-first/belief-second approach. But the task of reconciliation does seem to me to be *clearer* when we take a look at our behavior first. We simply learn more about what our motives truly are. In this book, and especially in this chapter about the "uses" of sex, I'd like to explore what it might be like to construct a moral system that actually *reflects* our behavior, a system that allows—even perhaps encourages—us to behave exactly as we *do* behave. I'm not saying that every belief we locate in ourselves will be so clear; in fact, you can count on discovering that your motives are almost always an ambivalent tug-of-war. But at least you'll better know what they *are*. You may find, as the above-mentioned HIV-positive man found, that your behavior isn't after all giving you what your forceful motives (the basis of your beliefs) now make it clear you want. Changing behavior because it's not giving you what you really want is much more practicable than changing behavior because you think it's "bad." When you change out of desire for the change, rather than white-knuckling yourself into a change for some imposed moral reason, the change has a better chance of taking root.

Which brings us to another dividend of the behavior-first/

belief-second approach: looking at your behavior without flinching better enables you to see and understand its payoffs. Why do we act, sexually, the way we do? What are we after? What is our gay Republican really looking for when he goes to Afro-diziak? What are, after all, the uses of sex?

These aren't as obvious as they may first appear—even if some of them may seem so obvious as to be foregone.

BOYS JUST WANNA HAVE FUN

During my last bachelor sexual-smorgasbord period, I rented a room in a house in the Pines, in Fire Island. On the ferry on the first of the June Tuesdays I went out there—my life as a freelance writer allowed me the luxury of going out on weekdays—I caught the glance (after catching the sight of two incredibly beautiful muscular legs ending in thick white socks and tan construction boots) of a bearded man whom I judged to be roughly my age. Sparks flew. Whatever magical X-factor constitutes sexual interest exploded between the two of us so suddenly that I was made breathless by it. By the end of the boat ride, we'd exchanged first names and I'd invited him to see my house, which, as it happened, was right across from his. We began the tour in my bedroom. We were in each other's arms, our mouths over each other's bodies, our shorts and T-shirts shed fumblingly fast, wrestling, writhing over each other on my still-stripped bed, aching to find some adequate way to consume each other as completely as we could. We ended up beating off, kissing, licking, holding, and grabbing each other, like two young Labradors just come to puberty. That was it: it was an animal coupling—as awkward and urgent as teenagers, apes, dogs. After the incredible conflagration, as we lay in each other's sweaty embrace after coming, I think we both felt an almost complete moment of peace.

He said, *"Jesus,* I'm glad I'm gay." I agreed I was just as glad I was.

We got up, naked, trotted out to the pool, and both dived in. As we floated in postorgasmic bliss, we talked. Steve was a gardener; he came out on weekdays to take care of the grounds of the house he was staying in—this barter arrangement gave him a room for the summer.

"I have a lover in the city," Steve said.

"Does he know about your extracurricular activities?" I asked.

"Well . . ." Steve hesitated. "Probably. But we don't talk about it."

"Does he fool around, too?"

"Yeah, I think so."

This exchange is so classic it's a cliché: it describes (to some people's dismay, to others' acceptance) the tacit situation of so many gay men: fooling around on the side; not talking about it to the significant other. One more bit of evidence, to those looking for it, that few gay men are capable of sexual fidelity. But I sensed something in Steve's tone that was so free of conflict—there wasn't the slightest tremor of defensiveness or guilt in him—that I wanted to pursue what it was in him that made him feel so conflict-free. I felt he'd somehow passed a hurdle that not many other gay men have been able to jump: it really *was* okay that he and his lover fooled around "on the side." He seemed not to be plagued by the least bit of discomfort or jealousy. Was it an act?

"It's just this," Steve said when I asked him how he'd managed to be so comfortable with this arrangement. "My lover and I decided very early on that being two men in a marriage couldn't ever be like being a man and a woman in a marriage. I mean, for whatever reasons, the men he and I are—the men we can't help being, don't want to stop being—are sexual adventurers and predators. Sex, to us, is plain damned fun. We both love the hunt and the chase. We both love variety. We also love each other, we're emotionally committed to each other, we live well with each other—we're comfortable enough with each other—that sex on the side just isn't a big deal. It would be as foolish to stop having this fun just because we were married as it would for him to stop ordering take-out Chinese because I liked pizza. There's no reason we can't have both."

"Then why don't you tell each other what you're doing?"

Steve laughed and shook his wet, curly head. "Well, we're *human*. I mean, I don't want to know details, and he doesn't either. I'm not saying we're incapable of jealousy. It doesn't thrill me to imagine he's going to bed with some Adonis with a ten-inch dick. I mean, I've got my physical vanity. But emotionally—we trust each other not to hurt each other. What we're doing works for us."

"What about AIDS?"

"Did you and I do anything you'd call unsafe?"

"No."

"That's your answer. I don't fuck without a condom. I'll suck dick"—I could attest to his expertise—"but I won't swallow come. That's risky to some people, but not to me—and apparently not to you either. I mean, you take what risks you're comfortable with. My lover and I protect each other in ways we've mutually agreed on."

This all seemed somehow too good to be true. I felt as if I were watching a boy from that island of self-indulgent kids in Disney's *Pinocchio:* where were his donkey ears? But as Steve floated, smiling, stomach-up in the pool, his dark curls spreading in the rippling water, his hairy chest glistening, his languid cock and balls floating, gleaming wet in the sun, I saw the picture of a man completely at peace with himself. He had constructed his life to give him what he needed and wanted. He had found a partner who had (evidently) constructed his life similarly. Neither one was turning into a donkey.

I have no doubt that darker currents plague Steve and his lover; I have no doubt there were deeper and more mysterious motives in him than the one he articulated for me: "Sex is plain damned fun." But he wasn't faking some basic comfort with himself, and it awakened a realization in me. I was not in love with Steve; it would be nice to see each other again, but it would be fine, too, if we didn't. Our sudden tryst was complete in itself. It needed nothing else, no follow-up, no rationalization, no hastily constructed context, to make it seem all right. We were two kids playing. We were a gay Huck and Tom: "Come out to the raft, Huck honey," and Huck did.

Sex can be this kind of uncomplicated fun. It is my contention—one only whose barest outlines I will reveal here (it will grow into a stronger theme later on)—that Steve's assertion that he and his lover were "men" is richly telling. Through whatever confluence of nature and nurture, many—I would venture to say most—men, straight or gay, have a predatory impulse, an instinct for variety, an ability to pursue and have sex as a sectioned-off experience, one that need not plunge them into undue despair, guilt, or longing. Sometimes sex is, as it was for Steve and me this June morning, like Huck and Tom on the raft.

Again, for whatever innate or cultural reasons, men, far more than women, do seem to have this propensity to fuck because it's fun. Don Symons, an evolutionary psychologist who, as William Allman says in his fascinating book *The Stone Age Present,* has long studied the evolution of human sexuality, is quoted by Allman to this effect: "Heterosexual men would be as likely as homosexual men to have sex most often with strangers, to participate in anonymous orgies in public baths, and to stop off in public rest rooms for five minutes of fellatio on the way home from work, if women were interested in these activities." But most women are not. Because gay men have other men as their sexual objects—many of whom, by the evidence of all those listings in *Next* and *HX,* are very happy to meet each other briefly, casually, anonymously, and frequently—the Huck-and-Tom model of sexual coupling is a familiar and, sometimes, a very satisfying one.

I will, as we go on, gently put forward more evidence to this end—that simply by being men, we have predictable sexual capacities and propensities that may partly explain our frequent sexual voraciousness. But Steve brought this home to me in a very personal way. I realized, floating beside him in the pool, that fun was an entirely adequate use for sex: it didn't *have* to be more. It certainly *could* be more, but it didn't have to be. I realized something I was already on the road to understanding: the guilt we often felt after a Huck-and-Tom experience such as the one I've described is sometimes a vestigial reflex, a sort of psychological "tic" left over from some internalized message we'd gotten from Mommy, Daddy, our fourth-grade teacher, Father Donnelly, or Rabbi Schwartz. Sometimes, of course, it's more—guilt is not always bad; it can be a warning sign that we're not attending to some deeper need or desire, that we're violating a more important pact (with ourselves or another person) than the sex we're having.

But I had no need for guilt: I wasn't attached to anyone with whom I had a pact that outside sex would endanger. And Steve, as we've seen, was behaving in alignment with his own pact. Sex was what I now realized we could let it be: fun. There was nothing demoralizing or dehumanizing about it. Far from it; it was hot, it was satisfying, and it connected me with an unmistakable sense of joy.

SEX AS PHYSICAL DISCOVERY

Kevin is five feet eight inches and just under three hundred pounds. He is, in his own word, "huge." But he likes himself huge. "I think I'm sexy," Kevin says. "Not that I always did. I mean, I grew up in the same culture you did. Nobody has to tell you how obesity is regarded in America—it's a sin almost as bad as being gay. I've been through all sorts of self-esteem shit over this, and all sorts of therapy, all kinds of diets that haven't worked. But, I'll tell you, about a year ago, at the baths, sitting in my dimly lit room, naked on my cot, stroking my dick, I suddenly looked down at myself—something I usually tried to avoid doing because the sight of my own body had always disgusted me—and, I don't know, there was something about my hairy chest and big stomach and fat, hard dick, bushy pubic hair, nice heavy balls, nicely shaped, if huge, thighs—anyway, I actually found myself *hot.*

"I'm pretty sure about what kicked this off. There's this guy I only see at the baths—it's an amazing place to me, the baths, like some kind of limbo-land where it's always three in the morning, and people move around like visions in a dream, it's incredibly unreal, and I love it, makes me feel like I'm in some giant womb, maybe—anyway there's this guy I only see at the baths, we've never exchanged names, but he always comes in and has sex with me. You won't be surprised to hear how rare it is for some normal-sized guy to take an interest in someone like me. But this guy's actually cute, in the conventional slim-hipped sort of way. He'll come in wordlessly, shut the door behind him, drop his towel, and stand in front of me to be serviced. I love sucking his dick. He's always a little sweaty, like he just worked out. He smells like a man—like I imagined the high-school jocks smelled, those untouchable perfect football players I used to envy when I was in school. Not that this guy looks all that much like an athlete. He's just a regular slim guy. But we'll get into a rhythm sometimes—it's like we'd rehearsed some incredible dance and we'll just start getting into it, wildly, perfectly—*God, it's wonderful!* And just before he comes, he'll jerk his dick out of my mouth and beat off all over my chest, while I beat off in unison. And he'll always say the same thing at the end: 'Thanks. That was hot.'

"But this time, a year ago, when we went through our usual dance—it was if anything better than ever—we both came, he sat down on my bed, leaned back on the wall, cupped and fondled my balls with his right hand, and said something I'd never in my life heard before. 'You know,' he began, 'you're one of the hottest guys I've ever had sex with in my life.' "

Kevin at first dismissed this as the ravings of some lunatic who perversely got off on fat guys. "I secretly was thrilled, but it took a long while before I could really register that someone might actually find me hot. I mean, I've always been a good cocksucker: I guess I felt I had to be, to compensate for how I look. Might as well have *some* expertise gay men were interested in. But this was different. This moment, I mean, of looking down at myself and accepting, liking, even loving, what I saw. It was like the first moment in my life where I'd enjoyed being a physical being. Something released in me. Now, when I'm home, like after I take a shower, I'll stand in front of the mirror and caress myself, tickle my nipples, stroke my balls, and masturbate. I'll get off on my own body. And I'm still as fat as ever. But, for the first time, I accept that I'm *here*. And I *like* that I'm here—I even get off on it. What does that mean? Who knows? Am I some kind of weird narcissist? Maybe. But I feel a lot better now than I did when I couldn't stand the sight of myself."

There's an odd disjunction in much of gay male experience: while the gym has become as sacred and important an experience to gay men as church is to nuns, few gay men I've talked to have much physical self-acceptance. The Body, as purveyed by The Gym, is like an Armani suit that takes money and untold hours of discipline to earn. It is something acquired—something almost external to the being acquiring it. The physical self-acceptance Kevin is talking about is much more basic and satisfying. And sex can be a wonderful way of finding it.

Sex gives gay men—so many of whom spent their boyhoods not feeling physically adept, not being athletic, not quite believing they *existed* physically—an arena to discover their physical selves. That this discovery often has the trappings of delayed adolescence—the haughty attitude with which we judge each other physically is just as harsh as that of any junior-high jock picking members of a softball team (and not picking you)—is perhaps understandable: we are, in the sexual arena, often acting out a social, emotional, and physical adolescence we never had when we were fourteen. But we can grow beyond that attitude and take more joy in our physicality. Doing this seems to me to be an underexplored "use" of sex for gay men: the way it provides us some sort of contact with, and acceptance of, our bodies. We have the opportunity to learn in sex that that we *exist*.

We usually learn this slowly. Sometimes, as Kevin said, we may start out by only being able to accept we have this or that expertise, that we are physically useful, viable, attractive, only in a certain light and under certain limited circumstances (Kevin's: "It had to be dark, and I had to have my mouth open"). But this acceptance can widen to a healthier self-love; in fact, achieving the kind of narcissism that Kevin describes is real progress.

I applaud the narcissistic urge in so many gay men: we *need* to love ourselves, to get off on ourselves, to find ourselves absolutely, physically, sexually wonderful. It is a necessary antidote to the lack of self-acceptance, the out-and-out self-hate, that crippled so many of us growing up. Sexual exploration can be an important means of finding this necessary self-love; learning that our bodies are more than Armani suits, that they are the full, mysterious, interesting physical manifestation of who we are—this is a heady discovery.

I have a German friend who invited me on a trip to East German shortly after East and West Germany reunified. He took me to a tiny island in the Baltic called Hiddensee. It was mid-September; the gray, cold northern-European autumn was already rolling in. But being German, he—and his countrymen who were likewise vacationing on this tiny island—were determined to strip down and stride into the Baltic as if it were summer and the water weren't freezing. The water *was* freezing, but enough of me was German not to want to be left behind; so, every day, rain or shine, my friend and I stripped and strode into, and experienced the shock of, the September Baltic Sea.

It was magnificent. Despite the inevitable shrinking effect on genitalia of freezing ocean water, I had never felt so powerful, so physical, so *male*. I was conscious—with a variety of other naked men and women, of all ages, shapes, and sizes around me—that I hadn't the tiniest fear of being judged as less than Apollonian. Some spirit was unleashed in me, and in my friend, that D. H. Lawrence would have applauded: we felt for this moment free, virile, *complete*. But what most stays with me is how much of a physical male *animal* I felt.

It made me wonder: is this what straight boys felt, growing up in a culture that loved them, straight boys who could throw footballs and catch baseballs, straight boys whose sexuality was applauded by every ad for breath mints and beer (not to mention their parents and teachers and friends and coaches)— was this sudden physical acceptance of myself as a man what a heterosexual man felt continually, as a matter of course, growing up, applauded for growing up, straight?

I know that this is too simplistic a comparison—plenty of straight men feel inadequate about their bodies—but the sheer newness of this physical self-acceptance was overwhelming, and it flooded me with questions; and made me realize, as I thought of the gay men I knew, how rare it was for gay men to feel it. Sex (which I had every day with my German friend after each plunge into the Baltic) becomes, in the wake of this self-acceptance, an entirely new experience. Sex is a *freedom* when you know that you are physical—not some sort of odd and cumbersome performance that you must do right and look right doing to succeed. You do not need to wear an Armani suit to have sex. You can be as fat as Kevin. Or as shrunken—and happily naked—as my friend and I were in the cold Baltic Sea.

SEX AS BUNGEE JUMP:
TESTING LIMITS

The lessons of the seventies—when it was politically correct to have sex with as many men as you could—changed gay male sexual behavior forever. I'm not sure that the ingenious variety of our sexual fantasies changed or grew; but, without doubt, our experience of *acting* on those fantasies burgeoned beyond calculation. Despite the plague of AIDS, this sexual ingenuity has in no way diminished. We may be changing certain practices, but if anything that seems to have spurred greater and more imaginative sexual exploration—and sexual self-acceptance. I remember, in the early seventies, creeping with extreme trepidation into the leather bar the Ramrod in the far

West Village of Manhattan. The black-clad men there were unimaginably sinister-looking—a weird and alien minority who indulged, tantalizingly, in God knew what. I was afraid to look any one of them in the eye: who knew what hypnotic power they might have over my naive self?

Today, a bar called the Lure—also a leather bar—is one of the most popular in New York, packed every night with gay men who seem far more a part of the mainstream. Its atmosphere is no longer frightening; no longer is the phenomenon of sado-masochism so foreign or forbidding—or perhaps taken so seriously. The men in the Lure seem to realize they are playing roles, moving in and out of them with greater comfort and self-acceptance and even humor than ever before. The inner, forbidden Hieronymus Bosch landscape of what was once considered far-out sex has, in many ways, now become an actual three-dimensional playground we've learned we can play in without growing donkey ears.

Partly fueled by the sexual taboos AIDS has placed upon us, more and more gay men are devising imaginative ways to get off that don't involve the ingestion of bodily fluids. Special-interest gay sex groups have multiplied: you can now find hordes of men into socks, boots, underwear, bondage, water sports, wrestling, cross-dressing, hot wax, rubber, a variety of sexual toys (tit clamps, dildos, harnesses, etc.). Perusing the personal ads in gay magazines takes you on a fascinating sexual odyssey. A random sampling of personal-ad headlines from our old standbys *Next* and *HX:* "Military Guys Wanted," "Lycra Spandex Fetish," "My Butt, Your Fist," "Red Hot Spanked Buns," "Turned on by Boxing?," "Clipper Haircuts," "Let's Play Ball" (from a Yankees-fixated man), "Are You Wearing Business Socks?," "Belly Button Massage," "Hot Nipple Action," "Hot Piss Slave Seeks Master"—well, you get the picture.

More to the point, you are very probably part of the picture—in a way most of your preseventies forebears couldn't dream of being. George Chauncey's wonderful book, *Gay New York: Gender, Urban Culture, and the Making of the Gay Male World 1890–1940,* makes it clear that gay men's sexual explorations and ingenuity are far from new; but perhaps the most stunning impact of the book for me is the force with which it reminds me how new our current sexual visibility is. We'd have been peremptorily arrested and locked up for the kind of sexual advertising and play many of us now do without blinking. Not, God knows, that men still aren't locked up for sodomitic "crimes," or that we no longer live in a homophobic society. But we still have sexual license that would have been unimaginable to the gay man of only twenty-five years ago. That sex ads like the ones I've cited fill the backs of so many gay magazines tells us we're in an astonishing new age.

It also clarifies what I think has become one of the most fascinating and rewarding uses of sex: in this vast playground we've constructed for ourselves, we've pushed the envelope of what's possible—I maintain not only sexually, but imaginatively, personally. Through all this ingenious sexual play, we're discovering we can be many, many selves. There is, at least potentially, a wonderful widening of identity that all of this sexual play enables us to find and explore. I would say more: for many gay men, the acting out of formerly taboo or shameful sexual fantasies has been profoundly healing, therapeutic.

The most dramatic instance of this I can think of is Dirk. Dirk now lives with a lover, Joe, which is an accomplishment he once thought impossible. "From my teen years to about age thirty," Dirk said, "I was a multiple personality. I had about twelve people inside me. Everyone from Hank, a total sexual renegade, kick-ass leather biker top, to Edward, a bookish, sweet, self-effacing boy who stammered and was afraid of everything. I also had a couple of women: Ann, a prim and efficient secretary type, and Lucy, a giggly and flirtatious teenager who was always thinking about boys. Then there was this jock type named Jim (he watched a lot of football on TV), an alcoholic named Phillip who probably got me into my worst trouble—he'd get into blackouts and end up breaking store windows or getting on planes to Mexico City—and a number of others who popped up less often who filled out the spectrum. There was even a straight guy named Jack who would go to singles bars."

Dirk seemed, to me anyway, to have coalesced, and he agreed that he'd been able to find the true, integrated self he called Dirk with the help of his lover, Joe. "Joe actually met the biker 'Hank' at a leather bar in Folsom Street in San Francisco and took Hank home with him. Hank was a pretty forbidding character, but Joe seemed to understand that the tough and sadistic front was, in fact, a front. Most men Hank met were freaked out by him—I'll tell you why in a moment—and high-tailed it away from him, but Joe decided to stay. It was a turning point for me, Dirk—and 'Hank' as well.

"When these personalities first started manifesting in me, they didn't know about each other's existence. But by the time I met Joe—I was about twenty-eight—they *did* know about each other, and in fact I'd been going, sometimes on court orders, to various shrinks to get cured—which meant work on getting to know them better, why I was splitting off like this, with the goal of finding one personality I could depend on. But nobody helped me like Joe did."

"Hank" was so frightening to most people who met him— even to Dirk—because his sexual tastes were so wild, even gory. "Thank God he never became another Jeffrey Dahmer," Dirk says, "but he was into dismemberment scenes—he got off on the idea of some kid being drugged and strung up in a basement, slowly tortured, burned with cigarettes, stabbed with knives, and finally cut open and apart. Hank would create these incredible verbal scenes while he straddled whatever sexual partner he'd gone home with, going into graphic detail about the imaginary kid getting dopier and dopier from the drugs and getting slapped and punched and kicked, savoring each detail of blood spurting up from each imaginary wound. Even guys into the far reaches of sadomasochism would often be grossed out—or scared out of their wits—and get away from Hank as quickly as they could. I think, actually, that might have been Hank's more or less secret intent—to scare them so they'd leave. Maybe he did this so he wouldn't end up actually acting out the gory scenarios. I don't know."

But Joe, subjected to Hank, didn't bolt. In fact, Dirk/Hank says, "He asked me questions about it. He took Hank seriously. He actually turned Hank's sexual monologue into a conversation—something that had never happened to Hank before." Hank did something he'd never done in a sex scene: "He turned into the sweet, stammering, shy Edward. I'd never moved from one personality to another in front of a sex partner before," Dirk says. "But Joe saw me do it. And while I'm sure he was freaked, he still didn't leave. He had the instinct just to talk and listen to Edward, as intently as he had with Hank. I know this began some sort of major shift in me. It was, I guess, like discovering that I could actually be more than one self with another person. I suppose on some obvious level—this has come up in therapy a lot—I was resorting to all these disparate selves to act out feelings I didn't think I was allowed to act out as 'one' person. But Joe, from the first night I met him, began to show me that I could be more 'selves' without whoever I was with leaving me."

But there was something even more healing about Joe, Dirk says. "He shared some of the same sexual fantasies that Hank—and I—had. He was this example to me, I guess: he could have these gory, sadistic scenarios in his head, in his fantasy life, without being scared to death of them—without resorting, as I had, to the desperate tactic of creating a whole, separate cutoff character into which I could dump all those frightening feelings. He could have scary and exciting thoughts without ripping himself apart—he could still be *Joe* and have them. I never knew this was possible—and I'd certainly never met anyone who'd been capable of this."

Joe seemed to act as a catalyst for Dirk to "find" Dirk. "Meeting Joe all happened in the context of therapy. I would take this new and frightening idea that maybe I might, after all, be able to be Dirk—and have the feelings, desires, thoughts, fears, hopes, and dreams of Hank, Edward, Phillip, Lucy, Ann, and all the rest of them—to therapy to talk about, get more comfortable with. Within a year, some magical coalescing happened—and I became the singular person I am now."

Just as healing, Dirk says, is the sexual relationship he has with Joe. "Joe has encouraged me to give full vent to my sexual fantasies. We've rigged up this 'torture chamber' in one room of our apartment. It's lit by red light, has a rack, a full set of metal constraints and chains, a pile of pornography—videos of particularly way-out SM scenes. We're into threesomes or even larger groups. We advertise on phone lines, on the Internet, in *Drummer*. I've got this scrapbook full of really gory stuff for guys we think won't be freaked out by it, and I'll get turned on doing what Hank used to do—talking about it, while I slap another guy or put clamps on his nipples, beating off. We make sure the guys we meet are really into it. Joe's there getting off on it, too, which reassures, comforts me, I guess. The group scenes don't always work out, but when they do, I can't tell you—it's incredible. I feel the most amazing explosion when I ejaculate—I have the idea that all those former selves, even prim secretarial Ann, are somehow cheering me on, telling me it's okay to feel what I'm feeling, to go over the top, to *be* this wild, sexual self. I learn from these experiences that I won't blow up or die or descend into hell, by giving expression to this dark sexual part of me. I feel more complete at the end, not less."

Dirk has described what he freely admits is "the ideal experience. I mean, sometimes, when it doesn't work out, it can feel empty—even sort of horrible. But not so horrible that I hate myself. Joe is still with me—it's like he keeps reassuring me that whatever I'm feeling is okay. I don't have to turn into someone else to escape it."

We are in delicate, charged territory. A part of pushing the envelope in the sexual arena means discovering and exploring what might accurately be called the psychosis of sex. The inner landscape of sexual fantasy is fiercely compelling—it has its own rules, it is timeless, it can be so absorbing that no other part of life has any reality in it. This is the true danger (and excitement) of sex: this is, in fact, the "volcano." Dirk needed Joe—and therapy—to begin to explore this territory without bolting into some other character for safety. There's no guarantee that another man, torn by the fantasies that impel Dirk, might not have become another Jeffrey Dahmer. The boundaries between fantasy and acting out the fantasy can sometimes blur so completely that you behave disastrously.

But sometimes, when we can find, as Dirk found, a "Joe," some agent—a real person (therapist, friend, lover) or even a new, firmly rooted self-affirming attitude—that tells us our sexual fantasies do not automatically label us "sick," that they can be enjoyed as fantasies, do not have to be acted out completely to be enjoyed, we can enter, as Dirk has entered, a new realm of freedom. The question of the morality of a fantasy is moot: fantasies, like dreams, are complicated and involuntary condensations of our fears, drives, wishes, defenses—they don't care whether you approve of them or not. They'll be there anyway. By accepting his fantasies, and even by enjoying them more, Dirk is learning that he can after all contain them. "It goes beyond accepting the

'Hank' feelings in myself," Dirk says. "My whole life isn't sex. All the other selves I once resorted to are just as true about me. I am all the feelings that once made up Lucy and Ann and even that straight guy, Jack. What's opened up for me isn't only a new permission to have and to some degree act out on my sexual fantasies. I feel, more and more, like I've got a new permission to have all my other feelings, too—all the gentle, doubting, hoping, funny stuff that my other personalities once gave voice to."

Later on in this book we'll go deeper, speak with men who've more completely explored what their fantasies tell them about who they are and what they most fundamentally want. Sometimes giving voice to the motives that fuel fantasy ends up—usually very slowly—changing the fantasy. It may be worth pursuing this shift more consciously, with psychoanalytic and perhaps medical help (about which more in chapter 4), if the fantasy is overwhelmingly self-destructive or threatening to anyone else. But what Dirk has done sets the stage for this deeper exploration, an exploration that can only happen in the context of *permission*—letting yourself be who you already are.

SEX AS EMPLOYMENT: HUSTLERS AND JOHNS

Ricky is a twenty-four-year-old bike messenger who looks *incredible* in bike pants: slim, with pale blond hair and deep-set gray eyes, he simultaneously conveys the vulnerability of a boy and the virility of a full-grown man: sleek, lithe, tightly muscled torso; heart-stopping bubble butt; and a pornographically bulging jock. "I love being a bike warrior," Ricky says, "all that stuff you hear about us being the new adventurers—sort of like cowboys in the Old West. But I also love the *attire*. I mean,

I know I look good in it." Ricky smiles meaningfully as he gazes down at his explicitly outlined crotch, tight and fat in his bike tights. "I get off on making people crazy. You should've seen the look on the face of the CEO whose office I just came back from. I was supposed to give this package to his secretary, but he walked out of his office while I was there and I thought he'd have a heart attack when he laid eyes on me. I know plenty of guys like him—a lot of them married, straight, and conventional in a business suit, but who go nuts when you get them in a hotel room. I didn't say a word—I just handed him my card."

Ricky's card had nothing on it but his first name and a beeper number. "I expect him to call any minute," he said.

Ricky became a prostitute almost from the moment he came to New York, three years ago, after "escaping a small town in Pennsylvania where gays were hated more than rats. My mom and dad are real conservative, to put it mildly, and I think they were as glad to get rid of me as I was to get rid of them." Once in New York, Ricky quickly got his bike messenger job and began at once to see that he could turn the looks he was getting into fairly big bucks. "I guess I was new, fresh meat," Ricky said. "I started hanging out at the 'boy' bars in the East Fifties and talking to some of the other hustlers, figuring out how to go about hustling. I never saw anything wrong with it. I mean, you had hustlers who liked to have sex for money and johns who liked to pay them for sex. Where was the problem? I didn't feel exploited. I was doing exactly what I wanted to do."

What Ricky hadn't wanted to do, however, was get the AIDS virus, for which he recently discovered he now tests positive. "I guess I'm one of those kids who never imagined they were mortal. I was also pretty stupid—I got high a lot when I first got here, really whacked out on MDA, Ecstasy, Special K, booze—you name it, I pretty much did it. And I *love* getting fucked. I mean, one of my favorite things is to keep a john waiting for it—making him nuts, getting *this close* to him, flashing my dick and my ass in his face, but telling him he has to keep his hands to himself. It's sort of like being top and bottom at the same time—I'd control the man until he was about to explode, like a top, but then I'd let him fuck me, like a bottom. Anyway, I'd really get nuts when I got high. And I didn't give a shit about condoms. I fucked pretty much everybody without one, unless he wanted to use it. That was pretty screwed up, I guess. But, hell, what can I do about it now?"

One thing Ricky is careful to do about it now is to let his potential johns know he's HIV-positive. "It's the first thing I tell them when they call me. I would say I screen out about two-thirds of the guys who are interested in me—they vanish, just like that, when they hear *this* little bit of news. The guys I meet know what they're getting into. It's not like you can't have sex with someone who's got HIV. When a guy fucks me now, he uses a condom. Most guys who meet me, if they want me to suck their dicks, won't wear a condom for that. That's their choice—it's fine with me either way. And some guys will suck my dick, too. I won't come in anyone's mouth, and I won't let anyone come in my mouth. But, you want to know the truth, I don't think *any* virus is ever gonna get gay men to stop sucking dick. But I'm honest. I'm not trying to infect anyone with anything. I'm just doing what I like doing, what I do best. This bike messenger thing keeps me in shape, and I love speeding through the streets of New York, pissing off cabdrivers and stuff. And it's a great way of connecting with hot-shit corporate types, like I did this morning."

Are there no down sides to any of this? "Of course," Ricky says. "Man, *I* should be the one writing your book. You can't imagine how many different types of guys I meet. You can't imagine what they tell me. You think you tell your barber or your bartender everything? That ain't shit compared to what you'll tell a hustler. I don't know, maybe they think I'm not listening, or I don't understand, or I'm just some blank thing they can dump everything out on. I don't mind. I'm just fascinated. But sometimes it's really sad. Like this guy in his fifties who sees me regularly. God, what a case. He's an Orthodox Jew, comes from some Hasidic neighborhood in Brooklyn, and he's married with about eight kids. He's absolutely petrified every time he comes over. He won't take off his clothes. He just asks me to strip in front of him while he plays with his dick through his pants. I can't even really tell if he ever comes. But by the end he's almost always in tears. Not great huge sobs, just silent crying. It's heartbreaking. He keeps saying, 'I shouldn't be here,' but he keeps coming back. I'd like to think coming to see me helps him in some way, but it's like the misery he's in is so great—I don't know what could touch it." Ricky is quiet for a moment. "There are other guys, too—guys with really weird fixations and stuff. Like I always have to wear a certain kind of socks, or see-through underwear, or keep my shirt on but take my pants off. One guy gets off on getting me to sneeze—he actually has this sort of joke-store sneeze powder which he'll sprinkle in front of my nose so I'll sneeze. Another guy—little man, with bright red, curly hair—barks like a dog when he comes. I've often wondered about that—it's amazing how many people get off on wanting to be treated like dogs. Then there'll be guys from Europe, like this one Englishman who got off on making me wear rubber pants and then peeling them off me. So many English guys are into rubber. What do they do to them over there?" Ricky smiles. "So many stories. The stuff they tell me. The married ones, how hard it is to keep lying to their wives. The lonely guys who've never had a lover, and who feel their only hope is to pay for some attention. One guy, who still lives with his mother—he's about forty-five—says I'm better than his shrink. So many stories."

How does Ricky view his future? "Hey, man, you take it

as it comes. Sometimes I'll wake up in the middle of the night in a cold sweat and think, 'Shit, I'm gonna die!' But then I think, we're all gonna die. I feel fine now. I'm not spreading AIDS around. I look good. I've got some friends. I got a life. I'm okay for the moment. I don't know what else I could ask for. Sure, I guess I'd like to make some real big bucks and set myself up somewhere, sometime, running a dance club, maybe. I always wanted to do that—be some hot-shit gay entrepreneur, the new Steve Rubell or something. Believe it or not, you make connections being a hustler, especially with the CEOs." His beeper beeps. "Speaking of which . . ." He says good-bye and leaves to call back this morning's potential conquest.

Klaus, fifty, a music professor from Germany (whose mother was English and who is fluent in the language), one of Ricky's clients when he visits New York City, was willing to give me his "john" side of the hustling story. "I like Ricky," Klaus says. "Apart from his obvious charms, I like that he knows what he's about. He's not a sad case to me at all. As for me—well, sometimes I see myself as a sad case, I suppose. But it's not because I have sex from time to time with rent boys. The sadness I feel is just a part of being human. We all want and need contact so strongly—and I have gathered what I think of as a bouquet of 'flowers,' different people in my life to help me to satisfy different aspects of this need for contact. I have musician friends with whom I play chamber music—I'm a pianist. I have a number of women friends with whom I'll spend weekends in my country house outside of Hanover because they're simply the most satisfying people I know to speak with, spend time with. I had a lover for ten years who died of AIDS, and I suppose it was his dying and his death which connected me most strongly with this sense of ultimate 'sadness' and loneness I feel. His irreplaceability—the fragility of life—well, I'm not the first person to experience this, but it has affected me profoundly. I have other friends, casual 'lovers' I suppose, with whom I explore various kinds of sexual and emotional intimacy. But it's as if each relationship is its own world, with many joys and discoveries, but also limits. I probably sound more philosophical than I mean to. All I'm saying is that I see all of my relationships as satellites—self-contained worlds I can visit for certain reasons and in which I can experience certain sometimes wonderful satisfactions—but in the end I know that I am alone. Sometimes this is depressing—at other times it simply seems like reality. Anyway, when the sexual urge is most imperious, I'll hire a man to satisfy it. Sexual hunger is simply one more kind of hunger to me. I see no reason not to respond to it directly. I don't know why so many people—I must say, so many Americans—are so appalled by the ancient profession of prostitution. Paying someone for sexual services seems to me eminently reasonable. There would not be prostitution if there were not some profound human need for it. It is simply a fact, and often, for me, a very pleasant and satisfying one. Some of this satisfaction comes, of course, from the feeling that if you're paying someone for sex, you can, as that American commercial for Burger King says, 'have it your way.' I know that some of the release in paying Ricky for sex is that, for that moment, it gives me a sense of 'owning' him, of a peculiar kind of power. But there are always other dividends, emotional dividends. How can you touch or be touched by another human being and not feel some kind of deeper union? Sexual hunger is not only for the release of orgasm—it is for the pleasure of human warmth, the touch of another vulnerable body. Something deeper always happens. Pleasure is such a wonderful and rare commodity in human life: why not find and enjoy it whenever and wherever you can?"

The picture of hustlers and johns Ricky and Klaus have painted is arguably a rose-colored one. There are many gaunt-eyed, driven, and profoundly unhappy men who pay or are paid for sex whose lives can be seen to be full of desperation and self-destruction (and often, in the case of hustlers, a lot of drugs). But there are, I would argue, just as many men who participate in these sexual negotiations with a fair degree of serenity and satisfaction. We are, once again, in volatile territory, because we are dealing with primal drives and, in the sense I've already put forward, "psychotic" inner landscapes that always have the potential to overwhelm their participants. The "power" Klaus speaks of—that because he is paying for sex, he can "have it his way"—can easily go over the line into abuse. But the *fact* of paying or being paid for sex is merely that—a fact. It is probably one of the most publicly underreported facts of gay male sexual experience. I would suggest that there is nothing automatically "wrong" or "bad" about this fact—more, that paid sex can meet and satisfy some portion of the eternal drive in us for contact and release, which goes beyond sexual to become human. Klaus gives eloquent expression to one of the uses paying for sex has for him: "How can you touch or be touched by another human being and not feel some kind of deeper union? Sexual hunger is not only for the release of orgasm—it is for the pleasure of human warmth, the touch of another vulnerable body. Something deeper always happens." Ricky calmly gives what seems to me a defensible rationale for offering his services: "You have hustlers who like to have sex for money and johns who like to pay them for sex. Where's the problem? I don't feel exploited. I'm doing exactly what I want to do."

A lot of gay men on both sides of the hustling fence seem to agree. Whatever we may think of it, the fact of prostitution isn't likely to change anytime soon. And because it isn't, at the very least we might examine it for some of the payoffs it seems to offer so many of us. Perhaps it doesn't need to be shrouded in so much secrecy and shame.

SEX AS INTIMACY:
BECOMING VULNERABLE

This use of sex as a means of becoming intimate with another human being requires defining *intimate*. The sweet, sentimental, sexless associations we often bring to the word *intimacy* are so charged with unexamined assumptions that they seem to me to render the word useless, even meaningless. We are so often told, explicitly and implicitly (by those sources and guardians of our superegos: family, church, and culture), that sex is only good or even acceptable when it's "intimate"—warm, cuddly, unthreatening (i.e., ball-less). As a result, we often feel we somehow have to stuff the primal vulcanism of sex, which is often not very nice, into a virtual nun's habit of intimacy. More often than not, it won't fit.

It isn't only Bible Belt conservatives who preach this sort of intimacy as the synonym for acceptable sex. So much advice in psych/self-help books, some of them addressed to gay men, preaches the same ultimately guilt-inducing message that there's only one kind of right sex—the intimate kind. Relationship guides preach a kind of middle-of-the-road morality that can be comforting to the degree that it reinforces familiar assumptions, old pillows of "home truths," but that can also be profoundly alienating to those of us who can't seem, however much we try, to bring the gay Roseanne-and-Dan model off. So many gay men berate themselves for not being able to sustain intimate relationships before they've really examined what they (each privately) actually mean by intimate—or even if they *want* to pursue and sustain such a union. We are, most of us, so unclear about our real desires, and so much the slaves of various superego ideals of what we're supposed to want. Relationship guides can reinforce this sense of inadequacy: we keep trying to follow their eminently compassionate and reasonable advice and end up (sometimes) back on our knees in a dark booth of the nearest pornographic bookstore. A cycle of self-hate is reinforced, and nobody's helped by it. "I'll take the stink of healthy sweat any day over the stink of the authoritarian language of contemporary therapy," says Camille Paglia (in a review of Samuel Fussell's *Muscle: Confessions of an Unlikely Bodybuilder* called "Alice in Muscle Land"). I'm with her.

All that said, the question—and our personal, idiosyncratic experience—of intimacy remains. What do I mean by intimacy—what have gay men taught me it means?

We are intimate when we allow ourselves to be seen, by someone else, psychically naked—when we offer ourselves *as we are*. Intimacy inevitably implies vulnerability: sharing with someone else parts of ourselves that we are normally afraid to share or feel shame about sharing. Intimacy is an unnerving baring of the soul. As we've seen in our exploration of previous uses of sex, it isn't automatically bad that sex, for gay men, isn't always (or even perhaps often) intimate. Sex can simply be fun, a game or a sport—there can be a lot of enjoyment in making an up-front, on-the-surface meal of each other's body. The "bungee jump" use of sex may take us deeper into a private sense of expanding limits. But expanding limits *with* someone else—achieving intimacy—has other, very rewarding dividends.

I've suggested that our narcissistic urges more than have their uses—they are to be applauded. Learning to get off on yourself is, to some degree, a necessary precursor to developing the ability to fully get off on somebody else. I've also suggested that discovering and accepting yourself physically leads to a new kind of freedom: when you joy in your own physicality, sex is no longer a contrived act that depends on putting yourself in exactly the right light and performing like a specially trained seal. It becomes an easier, looser, less self-conscious, and often more satisfying means of uniting with someone else. But even this doesn't quite constitute what, for example, Brad says he means about intimacy with his lover, Jim.

"I didn't realize until recently," Brad, thirty-eight, an aspiring artist who has worked out assiduously over the past ten years and has a nearly competition-level bodybuilder physique, "how much of my life—my assumptions, how I treated my lover, Jim, how I treated myself—was on automatic. In fact, I prided myself on how spiritual and 'in the moment' my approach to life was. I set aside time in the morning and night to meditate, I've even run groups for gay men on achieving self-acceptance. As much as I'm into the gym and keep up the discipline of workouts, I've never related much to the whole gay gym-clone culture. Sure, I find plenty of other guys hot, but I've never been comfortable with the way so many gay men compete with each other, try to one-up each other, treat each other with such attitude. Having casual, anonymous sex has never made sense to me. Part of it is, I don't know how to go about it. I came out late—at twenty-six—and I missed the whole seventies sex scene. I'm terrified of getting AIDS. While I hear that this or that sexual practice is safer, that's not enough for me. Who knows that the virus isn't mutating so that it can be caught more easily than anyone knows? But the basic thing is, I've never had the temperament for easy fast-food sex. I like getting to know someone first, and using sex as a way to share something deeper than lust. I suppose, in some way I don't like admitting even now, I always felt a little superior to all those guys I see at the gym whose lives revolve around the hot clubs and gay resorts like Fire Island or Provincetown. That always seemed exhausting and shallow to me. I try not to judge, but the truth is, I always felt I was more self-accepting and mature than all those driven guys. Maybe a little part of me was jealous. I just couldn't imagine how to bring a life like that off."

Brad has been with Jim for the past four years. "Jim is my second lover. When I came out, twelve years ago, I latched onto the first safe man I could find without really getting to know him first—I was so scared of whatever gay life meant that I needed someone to take care of me, I guess. That relationship only lasted a year. I'd dated a little—not much—between my first lover and Jim, but had otherwise pretty much kept to myself. My life was gym, working on my paintings, and doing a lot of mostly menial jobs—cleaning apartments, word processing, working as a waiter for catering firms. Secretly, I had a very grandiose dream, even a belief, that I'd be discovered one day—that my paintings would suddenly be snapped up by a major gallery and I'd become, overnight, the next Jackson Pollock. But nobody seemed very interested in my painting. I guess I shoved down a resentment about this, a resentment that fueled me burrowing more intensely into meditation and the gym, a feeling of anger and emptiness that made me want to do anything to escape—that led me, eventually, to hook up with Jim."

Outwardly, Jim was very different from Brad. "Jim is a very successful entertainment lawyer. He's five years older than I am, has no interest in working out, loves going to plays and concerts, is very sophisticated about the performing arts, but knows next to nothing about the visual. We met because he joined a gay meditation group I've been going to for a couple years. He said in that group that he'd felt he needed to go 'deeper' into himself than he had. He was curious about meditation as a way to do that. He's interested in spiritual stuff, and we hit it off first just by talking about what it means to develop a 'centered' self. He was curious about me, seemed to think—to my amazement— that *I* knew far more about self-acceptance than he did. He said

I radiated a serenity that he envied. I was amazed because he seemed to have worked out how to live in the world far better than I've ever been able to do. *He* knew something I didn't. He's a brilliant man, funny, wonderfully articulate, and money has never been a problem for him. It's just always come to him. Money has been the biggest drag in my life—I'm always scrambling to pay bills and rent. I guess the point is, we both felt each other had a secret the other wanted to learn."

Brad and Jim's friendship quickly warmed to the point where they were convinced they'd almost been destined to meet: "Talking with Jim was a revelation to me. We were yin meeting yang: complementing and filling out each other's personalities so perfectly, it seemed, that there was something mystical about it." Brad sighs and shakes his head. "I now see how desperate we each were to fall in love. We sort of talked each other into this 'perfect couple' out of the need to be part of a perfect couple. Not that our differences didn't coincide rewardingly—they did, and they do now. But I see now that there was a good deal of desperation behind it. We were determined to turn each other into a perfect partner."

Sex was satisfying in what Brad calls a "gentle but intense way. Jim is incredibly physically affectionate, and he seemed to take such delight in my body. He'd often say, 'I can't believe I have a lover like you. I'd always dreamed of what it would be like to make love to a man as beautiful as you—sometimes I can't believe that you could want me!' I'd reassure him that I found him just as attractive as he did me. But really I was getting off on being adored—I know that now. And, looking back, I can see that smoking pot helped us to keep the dreamlike, mystical way we felt about each other alive—and to keep me from admitting that, really, I *wasn't* all that physically attracted to him. We both liked to smoke dope before having sex. It was an incredible aphrodisiac. He'd always switch off the lights before we smoked—then he'd light a candle and quickly take off his clothes and burrow into bed, waiting for me to follow him. He wanted to watch me take off my clothes—and I got off on doing a striptease in front of him. There was something so incredibly arousing about me feeling like this good in front of him—the dope made it even more amazing. We'd almost literally go out of our minds with the pleasure of sex after that."

But Brad said he began to wonder why they only ever had sex in the dark. "I'm actually hornier when I wake up in the morning than I am at night. I love to stride around naked—the second I'm in my apartment, I strip off. Jim was, I saw more and more clearly as we went on, very insecure about his body. It was like he didn't want me to see it. It's true, he's not muscular. He's a little overweight. I started to resent the fact that he kept hiding himself from me—I don't think I ever saw him naked in the light in that first year. It began to rankle. What else was he hiding? Why didn't he accept himself more? Worse, and harder to admit, I started—even stoned—not to enjoy touching him the way I used to. I started to be annoyed at his softness. He could diet if he wanted to—he could go to the gym, couldn't he? I worked so hard to keep myself in shape—why didn't he? Slowly he just seemed more lazy to me. I started to turn off to him. Sex between us began to trickle down to about twice a week—way down from sometimes twice a night. He started to shut down as he felt my rejection of him. Our conversations weren't so terrific anymore. The differences between us seemed less like yin and yang and more like unbridgeable chasms. It's like, slowly, everything got infected with doubt and resentment. I became convinced he hated my paintings, that he thought I was a failure. When he'd talk about some coup at work, it seemed to me he was just rubbing it in that I wasn't as successful as he was. Because I made so much less money than he did, he was paying a higher share of our rent and bills. Did he think he owned me because he paid more? The resentment grew and grew—and got worse partly because we never talked about it. It was like this big black cloud expanding between us that we pretended wasn't there."

Brad had a moment of awakening, after this, which he said came from a frightening moment of "blackness." "About two years ago I came back from a particularly grueling apartment-cleaning job which took up so much of my day that I didn't have time to go to the gym. I could feel myself slipping into a blacker and blacker depression. Nothing in my life seemed to be working. I *was,* after all, what I secretly suspected Jim thought I was: an out-and-out failure. I'd never make it as an artist. I'd never have enough money—I'd always have to depend on someone like Jim. And was I any better at relationships? What Jim and I had once had now just seemed to be so much self-delusion. I wasn't attracted to him—not really. I didn't like so much about him—we just didn't have the same values. I was nearing forty—and trying desperately to hang on to my youthful body. But why? What good was it doing me?"

Alone in the apartment—it would be a couple hours before Jim would return home from his job—Brad decided to smoke some dope. "Unknown to Jim, I kept a small stash of pornographic magazines at the bottom of my hamper. Lately I'd been getting stoned and taking them out, beating off to pictures I found particularly hot. I smoked a joint and retrieved the most reliable of the magazines—an incredible spread in *Playguy* of this slim, tightly muscled, young Mediterranean type. I always got off on looking at him—imagining I was burrowing down into his crotch, nuzzling his dick and balls. He was really hairy—I imagined I could smell his sweat. It's amazing, smoking dope, how you can almost *enter* a pornographic picture—feel the skin, see way down deep into the eyes. I began to beat off, staring at the man's stretched-out, hairy form, wishing, wishing so hard, that suddenly he could pop off the page and be real, hold me, make love to me the way I yearned to be made love to by someone. The look in this young man's dark eyes—somehow, stoned, it seemed he could really see me. The strength of wanting him got so great that I started to cry. It wasn't anymore that I wanted his beautiful body—I wanted whatever was in those eyes. I wanted someone to *see* me. Suddenly, it wasn't even sexual anymore. I couldn't hold on to the sexual desire—I'd found a deeper longing inside me. Then I made a very strange connection. It sounds so Freudian now—but I can't tell you how new and strong this sudden realization was. I was looking into the eyes of my father."

Brad says that his father died of a heart attack when Brad was twenty. "I think he knew I was gay even though I hadn't come out yet. I always felt I'd somehow broken his heart—he always looked so sad when I was with him. He'd shut down when I walked into the room. It was unbearable—I couldn't stand being near him because he always made me feel like I'd let him down in some horrible way. Somehow the look in this porno stud's eyes was the look in my father's eyes—full of a deep sadness that reminded me, now, how much I loved my father. More than that—this is the Freudian part, I guess—how *attracted* I was to my father. When I burrowed in my imagination into the porno kid's crotch, imagined I could smell his male body, I was having, I now knew, a memory of burrowing, as a really little boy, into my father's lap. It was almost the only time I remembered that he was being affectionate with me, stroking my hair while I dozed off in his lap. . . . God—I can't tell you what this memory did to me."

Brad is silent for a long moment. "I got up—it felt like I was in a dream—and rifled through my papers in the bottom drawer of my dresser and finally found what I was looking for: a picture of my father when he was in his early twenties, right about when I was born. It was a head-and-shoulders shot taken at the beach. He was smiling, tan—because you couldn't see past his bare, hairy chest, he looked as if he might have been completely naked. I lay back down on the bed, held the picture in front of my eyes, and slowly beat off. I was crying as I masturbated, crying with longing for my father—this pent-up love and shame and longing somehow combined to give me the most intense orgasm I think I've ever had."

Right at this moment, Brad heard the sound of the door unlocking. He froze. Jim had come home early.

"I was still stoned—every reaction I had was magnified. I felt so utterly exposed—and ashamed. Jim just looked at me. He saw the come on my belly, he saw my father's picture. I'd already been crying, now I started to sob. There didn't seem to be anybody in my life who could possibly understand what I was feeling, what I'd just experienced. Jim would hate me now—finding me like this, I was sure of it. Wasn't this the sickest imaginable thing, getting off on your father? He didn't even know I had any pornography—that was spread out all over the bed, too. I felt as small and ashamed as I ever had when I walked into a room and found my father frowning at me."

But Jim didn't react in any way Brad expected. He walked over to the bed, sat down, and held Brad tightly. He spoke gently, soothingly, "Let's talk about this when you're not stoned, okay?" He stroked Brad's hair. "It's all right, nothing bad happened. It's all right." But Brad, so hungry for the real embrace of some actual human being, couldn't hold back. "I started, blubbering, to tell him all the stuff I'd been holding back in me, not just from him, but from myself. How much of a failure I felt. How self-hating I was. How I kept working on my body because I wanted *something* about me to be acceptable. How much I missed my father. How much I wished he'd known how much I loved him. How much I longed to feel his love for me."

Jim rocked Brad back and forth in his arms and let him

blubber and cry. After a while, Brad calmed down and fell asleep. When he awoke, the effects of the pot had worn off, and he got up sheepishly to join Jim, who was fixing dinner in the kitchen. "Jim smiled at me. He said, 'Looks like you had a breakthrough.' I knew somehow that he'd understood. Some wall had been broken down between us. But we didn't collapse into one of our old huggy, New Age 'Oh, God, we understand each other so well' embraces. Jim said he wanted to talk to me and listen to me. That it had been a long time since we'd done that. That, in some ways, maybe we'd never really talked or listened to each other."

The dam had dramatically broken for both of them. After dinner, Brad went into more detail not only about his pent-up feelings, love, and sadness about his father, but about his feelings for Jim. He admitted he'd gotten off on "being adored." He admitted his resentments. He admitted his loneliness and fears and doubts about his lack of success. He knew there was something almost sadistic in how he'd flaunted his worked-out body in front of Jim, almost to *make* Jim feel inferior. Then Jim began to talk, "it seemed," Brad said, "for the first time about his real feelings. How ashamed he was of his body. How guilty he still felt deep down about being gay—ashamed that, at the age of forty-three, he still hadn't come near to accepting himself. He admitted he'd put on a lot of the 'spiritual stuff' because he thought it was what I wanted of him—that I'd leave him if he didn't find some way to be my perfect partner."

The details of Brad and Jim's confessions are almost desultory in the telling, but their content isn't what's important. What was important, especially to Brad, is that "Jim saw me ripped open and didn't reject me. Some new level of being able to *be* with each other has slowly revealed itself to both of us as a result. It may be no more complicated than this: we don't lie so much to each other anymore. We don't need to."

The dam of their sexual distance has burst as well. "Jim makes a point of getting into and out of bed naked now—makes sure I'm watching him. He wiggles his hips, sometimes, as he sees my eyes follow his back into the bathroom. 'Nice ass, huh?' he'll say. I've now framed that picture of my father; it's over my desk." Brad closes his eyes for a moment, then continues, "We feel, more than ever, like two kids in a sandbox when we have sex. So much of the shame and hiding is gone. Now we make love in the light."

Had Brad or Jim been asked at the beginning of their relationship whether they knew intimacy with each other, each would enthusiastically have said yes. But what they both realize is that they'd simply *wanted* to feel intimate—completely accepted, in all their vulnerability—and had convinced themselves, out of the desperation of that desire, that they'd achieved it. Gay men obviously are no less prey to romantic "across the crowded room" assumptions of instant love than any other human being who's grown up listening to pop music lyrics. Gay men intimidated by the carnivorous urban sexual arena may be particularly susceptible to this means of romantic escape: Brad says this is one reason he was. But he and Jim hadn't really begun the work of achieving intimacy—not only through sex, but through acknowledging their true feelings to one another—until Brad's exposure, his session with his father's picture. It was being discovered at a moment Brad felt exceedingly vulnerable that led to the breakthrough Jim says Brad had—a breakthrough Jim eventually shared by revealing himself just as openly.

It may seem after all my warnings about making greeting-card associations with the word *intimacy* that I've described an instance of achieving it that would be right at home in a greeting card. Tenderness, kindness, patience—all these are byproducts of the closeness Brad and Jim have achieved with each other, and all are words we often automatically associate with intimacy. But they weren't achieved by wishing for them: they came first through a moment, in this case a chance moment, of self-exposure; then through the pain and courage of Brad and Jim's allowing themselves to be seen, and working through what they each saw and revealed. Sex can be an astounding arena for this kind of exposure because it is so primal an act and experience; it draws on our strongest drives, our most unconscious selves, and can lead to some of our most wrenching revelations. Ultimately we are infants in sex; behind the trappings of the most alienating black leather, sadistic master is the same force that got that master to cry, as a baby, for his mother's breast. When we use sex to explore intimacy, we are exploring the most basic and primitive parts of ourselves—hearts and flowers don't begin to describe the force of where this exploration might take us, or the depth of insight and attachment it can help us to achieve. Intimacy is pretty powerful stuff.

We've hardly exhausted the uses of sex. Indeed, it's a part of the task of the rest of this book, not only this chapter, to widen and deepen our sense of what sex can mean, where it can take us, what it can tell us about ourselves: its uses are a primary concern throughout. My intention has been, with the help of the men you've just met, to turn the prism on some uses formerly thought to be foregone or immoral or both—not to play devil's advocate, but to suggest that the beast we've been calling a devil may not be one after all. There are many more interesting creatures at work in our psyches and sexual behavior: devils and angels are only two minor orders among them.

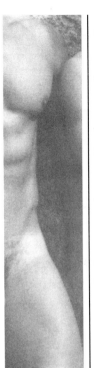

THE AMBIGUITY OF THE JOCKSTRAP

**GAY MEN
AS WARRIORS
AND SHAMANS**

THAT HEARING THE PARTICULARS OF gay male sex could be healing, that even the most allegedly "sordid" details could be accepted, learned from, and even enjoyed in a less consorious and more life-affirming way, is something I've been especially helped to do by Camille Paglia; for example, in her 1991 *Esquire* piece, "Homosexuality at the Fin de Siècle," where she recounts a moment of revelation about the promiscuity and anonymity of so much gay male sex:

> *One of the problems that most vexed me in my med-*
> *itation on sex is the promiscuity of gay men. Again and*
> *again, I was astonished to learn from gay friends of hot spots*
> *in notorious toilets at the diner, the bus terminal, or, Min-*

*erva help us, the Yale library. What gives? Women, straight
or gay, don't make a life-style of offering themselves without cost to random strangers in sleazy public settings.*

*At last, I saw it. Gay men are guardians of the mas-
culine impulse. To have anonymous sex in a dark alleyway
is to pay homage to the dream of male freedom. The unknown stranger is a wandering pagan god. The altar, as in
prehistory, is anywhere you kneel.*

The idea that kneeling before a hard dick can have almost
mystical significance is something most of us who suck cock
know from our own experience. Like most of the rest of sex between man and man, it's an amalgam of ancient childhood trance
(mouth on nipple, lost in the nourishment and unspoken physical connection of body to body), sexual fantasy that springs from
any number of historical sources, but perhaps most powerfully
the expression of one *male* making contact with another *male*. Gay
men are powerfully bound up in "the masculine impulse," "the
dream of male freedom": there are no easy dismissive ways to cat-
egorize or judge the lure of this impetus: we, like Paglia, often
find ourselves having to resort to mythical metaphors to begin
to convey the power and immersion of a man connecting sexually with another man.

Most people find Paglia controversial because of the arguably sexist male and female models she sets as the basis of her
critical thinking, most fully and provocatively in her magnum
opus, *Sexual Personae.* Indeed, some of the political gender-as-
destiny extrapolations she makes can seem questionable, even
silly. Applying what is essentially a literary discourse to politics
has a built-in untenability (D. H. Lawrence inspired the same
urge in his day, with the same impossible results): human beings
are not, after all, metaphors. But Paglia's unapologetic exploration
and celebration of the male and female archetypal differences she

sees are stirring, and potentially awakening—they can provide a richly illuminating metaphorical take on the pagan power, seduction, and sometimes brutality of sex. Exploring good old Western/Eastern duality with astonishing vigor and imagination, she draws some fascinating parallels from this exploration to what she sees as the pull in us between the hard-edged, leaping male Apollo, one of whose derivatives is the Warrior (my word), and the more female, entropic, sensual, "chthonian" Dionysus, from which derives the Shaman (her word). She challenges us to confront the sources of our sexual selves—a challenge I think essential for gay men to meet.

That her idea of male energy as a kind of Apollonian arc shooting up and away from the flood, muck, fertile chaos of Dionysus all seems to derive from biology—the sperm and the egg—makes her exegeses narrow, reductionist, and/or politically incorrect to her detractors. But we don't have to swallow all of Paglia to find her explorations illuminating, profitable. Her exhilarating metaphors can help us to see and appreciate the full spectrum of gay male passion, from the supermasculinity of the most brutal top to the androgynous beauty, danger, and mystery of the most feminine drag queen. She can allow us to see the power in our homosexuality, the power of men seeking men, evincing every gradation along this spectrum, in the context and quest of a purely homosexual freedom and identity, with all the terror and darkness and danger of this search as well as all the promise of light and freedom and discovery. Archetypes are, of course, symbols—not prescriptions for behavior. But they suggest, I think, some very potent truths about us nonetheless.

WHY WE SCARE STRAIGHT MEN

One thing is inescapably true: *there is no peace here*. There is discovery, sometimes; inexpressible elation, sometimes; terrible disappointment, sometimes; unbridled fury, sometimes; but there is no peace. More than that, the powerful archetypal urges that propel us are frightening in some very fundamental ways. Gay men are so threatening to the heterosexual male psyche because we seem, to straight men, to flaunt aspects of ourselves they have striven so manfully to suppress. This is never more the case than in the fact of our fucking each other. The idea of two men fucking scares the hell out of most straight men for some interesting reasons.

In *The Arena of Masculinity*, Brian Pronger's exploration of "sports, sexuality and the meaning of sex" as they relate to gay men, Pronger gets to the heart of this heterosexual male fear as he describes the jockstrap as an erotic symbol of both phallic power and anal receptivity:

> *The jock strap is perhaps the quintessential homoerotic ritual robe because, just as it enshrines the symbol of the myth of masculinity, so too the straps that originate in the top elastic circumscribe the buttocks and disappear at the anus, bringing us to that place where masculinity meets its mythic undoing.*

Gay men's symbolic "mythic undoing" of "masculinity" undoubtedly accounts for a good deal of the fear gay men engender in the heterosexual male, and the heterosexual male culture. Nowhere has this fear been more of a motive than in how the heterosexual culture has dealt with—or not dealt with—AIDS. In *The Culture of Desire,* Frank Browning has done a brilliant job of delineating the subtle and not-so-subtle homophobia (remember the word means *"fear* of homosexuality" not hatred of it) behind this reflexive connection. Our cultural heterosexual male taboo against anal penetration, which long predates AIDS, now has a whole new arena in which to assert itself. In fact, as Browning points out, although protected anal intercourse and fist-fucking present almost no risk of transmitting AIDS, many medical authorities have nonetheless preached a blanket taboo against any kind of anal sex. Paraphrasing U.C./Berkeley's neo-Freudian literary critic Leo Bersani, Browning tells us that this is because anal sex is profoundly unsettling to the heterosexual male: the "male's desire to be penetrated threatens to dislodge the phallic man, at least symbolically, from his position of authority." "The image of the insatiable gay man obsessed AIDS researchers, most of them straight men, in the early days of the epidemic," Browning says. "And it is the image they repeated over and over to the public: the men who had sex with ten, twenty, thirty men a night, hundreds a year, thousands per decade. . . . The promiscuous specter seemed monstrous to the researchers and to the public at large. Public-health officials, able only to consider viral and bacterial transmission, could come up with only a single response: Close the sphincter."

Most tragically this straight-male phobia about our sexual (anal) receptivity is one that gay men—brought up in a culture terrified of any sexual ambiguity—have themselves internalized. In the days of this epidemic, this internalized phobia—which amounts to self-hate—can have disastrous results, as Stephen Beachy's piece in *The New York Times Magazine* (April 17, 1994) attests. Beachy (a self-described member of the X generation who is "20+, HIV+, with 'no excuse' ") writes: "Maybe the image of death, a dark, sexy man in black, is something we find exciting. That's death as metaphor, of course, not sickness and putrefaction." It's too simple to say that Beachy got AIDS in "an age of safe sex, free condoms and fear" because he hated himself. No one's motives are that clear or simplistic. But Beachy offers himself as a kind of symbol of the new gay man who raises his middle finger to the general culture—and yet ends up killing himself. Somewhere here is the urge to self-destruct, an urge that his great gay grandfather Tennessee Williams knew intimately, an urge that Freud told us was as strong as the urge to live.

It seems urgent to me that we take a deep and close look at these archetypal motives, drives, expressions we find in our sexual selves to learn that we don't need to fear them—indeed, can develop a kind of behavioral power over, or at least pact with, them. *Accepting,* on the advice of Freud, that there are powerful libidinal (life) and aggressive (death) drives in each of us— accepting that some degree of wanting to self-destruct is as normal as the desire to live—can teach us that we don't have to be afraid of, or react blindly to, either of these urges. Death, as "a dark, sexy man in black," can remain a powerful metaphor, not a call to actually kill ourselves. It is possible, in other words, to accept the death drive without getting fucked by someone who's not wearing a condom because for an angry or despairing moment we've decided we've had enough and want to check out of life.

That's part of the aim of this chapter: to beckon to us to explore these sometimes frightening but compelling aspects of ourselves so that we not only awaken to their power, but to the exercise of choice we can develop in the rush of that power. But just as important an aim is to call for a fuller consciousness—even, when possible, an *enjoyment*—of these archetypal urges that kick, kiss, fuck, frighten, and caress us.

THE WARRIOR

Camille Paglia's *Esquire* piece cited above, "Homosexuality at the Fin de Siècle," partly inspires my choice of Warrior and Shaman as the quintessential gay male archetypes. She writes of "two principal kinds of male homosexuality":

> *The first and most ancient is rooted in identification with the mother, perceived as a goddess. The castrated, transvestite priests of Cybele, honored in disco-like rites of orgiastic dance, survive in today's glamorous, flamboyant drag queens.*
>
> *The second kind of homosexuality represents a turning away from the mother and a heroic rebellion against her omnipotence. Such homosexuality disdains femaleness and esteems perfected masculinity, which it symbolizes in the "hunk," the tautly muscular, arrogantly architectural male form first fully imagined by the Greeks. Greek athletics were a religious spectacle of the beauty of masculinity, formalized in the kouros sculptures that began the Western high-art tradition.*
>
> *There is nothing deviant or effeminate in this kind of homosexuality. On the contrary, I view the modern gay male as occupying the ultimate point on a track of intensifying masculinity shooting away from the mother.*

The "second kind of homosexuality" will concern us first: what I call the Warrior. I choose the aggressive word because it captures for me an essential lure of the archetype: it eroticizes the aggressive urge; it offers us a way to manifest, contain, and express our violent impulses, which I hold to be one of the most urgent tasks that face gay men.

I was riveted by an episode called "Sparring Partners" of the slapstick British sitcom *The Detectives* when it aired recently on a New York–area public television station. The two inept and idiotic eponymous police detectives of the show were instructed to infiltrate a local boxing gym to find out what dangerous drug was being administered to the gym's fighters—fighters who were all but killing their opponents in the ring. The superhuman strength and aggression of these bloodthirsty fighters turned out to be caused by a combination of testosterone and adrenaline— a Windex-looking blue liquid that, when ingested, revved up both the urge to fight and (although put less bluntly on the show) the urge to fuck. The premise was that, given a superdose of male hormone and adrenaline, a man could not control his aggressive or sexual urges—urges that fixated on whatever moving body was in front of him. The detectives accidentally consume the liquid and by the end struggle between wanting to kill and kiss each other. As they glared at each other with this split combination of sexual and murderous desire, they symbolized what seems to me to be our Western male society's greatest secret belief and fear: male hormones, cranked up sufficiently, engender the urge to fuck and fight *men*. In other words, out of control, men can be expected (as in prison) to become violent and homosexual.

President Clinton's attempt to allow gay men officially into the military caused such fear and outrage in many heterosexual men precisely because it threatened them with this assumed "inevitability." The idea of naked gay men in the showers, looking with lust upon naked straight men, in the context of the all-male military: how else to account for straight men's terror of this except to deduce that they imagine homosexuality, in all-male situations, to be on some level irresistible? Homosexuality is feared to be contagious because there is a powerful, repressed receptivity to it in straight men—a receptivity that has to be fought with every weapon at the straight man's disposal.

While this illuminates a core reason for homophobia, the fierce aggressive/sexual impulse in all of us also illuminates part of why so many gay men have fetishized the dangerous supermale: by seeking to become or be overcome by this macho man, we seek to give expression to our own volcanic "male" aggressions— aggressions with which many gay men grew up profoundly uncomfortable. I'm struck by another passage from Paglia's piece, about straight male teenagers' unruly development:

> *When I was young, I thought teenage boys were the most awkward, miserable, antsy, bratty, scuzzy, snickering creatures on God's green earth. Now at midlife and, as it were,* hors de combat, *I see them quite differently. Watching them rampage on the street or at the shopping mall, I find them extraordinarily moving, for they represent the masculine principle struggling to free itself from the woman's cosmic dominance.*
>
> *Teenage boys, goaded by their surging hormones (at maximum strength at this time), run in packs like the primal horde. They have only a brief season of exhilarating liberty between control by their mothers and control by their wives.*

Few gay men I've talked to ran "in packs like the primal horde" as teenagers. As children most of us seem to learn very early on to sideline ourselves from this chaotic male aggression: we read, drew, played music, dreamed—alone, or maybe with one other "best friend" (sometimes female). However, as we grow up and begin having sex with men—as we construct worlds that can accommodate our fierce, held-back sexual selves—we often find ourselves not in a "brief season of exhilarating liberty," which Paglia says limits straight male teenagers, but with the prospect ahead of us of a *lifelong* liberty. Freed from the constraints of having to marry, we're tempted by the lure, once again, of that Disney *Pinocchio* island of boys: we can now have as much fun as we want. The "primal horde" for gay men is the horde of the disco, the baths, the sex club, the dunes of Fire Island, the bushes of Golden Gate Park: here, finally, we can be as aggressively ruthless and posturing as any straight teenage boy in a gang. (Plus we get orgasms out of it!)

It is a heady and frightening freedom—and one for which we're profoundly unprepared. Long-repressed aggressions and sexual urges can propel us blindly into the horde—after what is often a lifetime of sexual and personal deprivation, it's no wonder that so many of us grab for as much of whatever we can, wherever we can. Add to this what I strongly believe is a natural, hormonal male predatoriness and you've got quite a chaotic sexual jungle. Add still further the now long-entrenched duplicity we developed to survive in the straight world—showing one face to the world, keeping another private (and often shameful) self to ourselves—and you've got the basis of cliché gay comedy: the forbidding black leather macho man at night who becomes a sweet, mild-mannered hairdresser by day. Gay men are societally propelled and hormonally impelled to be an incredibly divided bunch.

Given the tormenting pulls that besiege gay men, it's with real delight that I introduce you to twenty-three-year-old Jake, who demonstrates even in (what at age forty-five I consider to be his) extreme youth that we may, after all, be able to handle all these chaotic forces and even find great pleasure in them. Jake is a supremely self-confident Warrior who, as he says, can "get really close to the thrill of being a Warrior without doing myself in."

"I like the term *Warrior*," Jake says, "for a clear reason. I'm turned on by men fighting. I can't remember a time when I wasn't. Whenever my father would watch boxing or wrestling on TV, I'd be glued to the set—even as a five-year-old. I guess partly it was the only societally approved way for two men to strip down and get sweaty with each other. But there was also something about the sheer aggression which was the main turn-on. It's like, I can't believe boxing is legal: it's so incredibly sexual to me. I can't believe everybody doesn't see this. I mean, look at how two fighters stand next to each other at the beginning of a fight before the ref gets them to touch gloves. You see guys with their heads literally a fraction of an inch away from each other, staring into each other's eyes, close enough to kiss. To me, boxing-gloved fists are like dicks. Men fuck each other with their fists in a fight."

Jake's preferred scene, which he says he's acted out with a number of men he's met through personal ads, is to "strip down with a bigger guy and spar with boxing gloves. The thing that gets me hard is the idea of 'fighting for top'—but with the hope that the other guy will be stronger than I am and beat the fuck out of me. At the end, after he's beaten me into submission—in my fantasies this means getting knocked out, but in reality, it's mainly just me giving up when it starts getting out of hand and I feel like I can't take it anymore—I suck his dick."

Jake, who works in a bookstore and whom friends, family, and acquaintances know as a "quiet, studious type," enjoys the split between his public and his erotic personae. "I'm not eaten up by being two such different people," he says. "I sort of *love* it—I mean, I get a kind of thrill out of having this whole other sexual life that the people I work with don't know about. And, it's interesting, most of the guys I meet who are into this version of S and M have the same split. I mean, the most aggressive tops I've met are usually well-educated, nice, quiet guys who've got their shit together in their working public lives. I don't know, maybe to actually act this kind of stuff out, you have to figure out that it's okay to act it out."

A part of Jake's private erotic world is writing his own pornography. "I rarely find what turns me on in the gay male erotica you find on the magazine stands. I mean, I like a muscular guy with a big dick as much as the next gay man. But I like really tailoring pornography to my own tastes—which means, writing it myself." Jake recently wrote a piece he calls "Club Fighter," which he now shows prospective sex partner/opponents. "I can't believe certain guys' reaction to it," Jake says proudly. "I mean, they rub themselves raw over it. They can't believe somebody else thinks like they do." He was a little embarrassed to show it to me—"It's pretty off-the-wall, brutal stuff," he said—but finally relented.

I found its brutality fascinating (as well as erotic): it takes you right into the mouth of the volcano. An excerpt:

> . . . I start throwing for real now. Banging him around the fuckin' ring, then slamming him against the ropes so he can't fall. Plowing a right, a left, a right, into his gut; he covers up, then tries to clinch—I let him hang on to me for a second so I can smell his fuckin' sweat again—then start working over his head with picture-perfect lefts and rights— his head is now flipping back with each punch, sweat flying, blood from his brow and nose and mouth splattering my sweaty chest and my fuckin' underwear. But the fucker is still throwing punches, even if he can't land any. I plow a nice right into his gut, bring him up short with a solid left then right to his jaw, pump away at his fuckin' puffy red face. . . . He starts to slide down the ropes, tries to clinch, and ends up sliding his front down my chest, my chest hair matted with his sweat and blood, his fuckin' pathetic mouth sliding down my hard belly and over the fuckin' huge lump

in my shorts. Yeah, I think, I might find out what kind of cocksucker this piece of shit is after I'm through with him.

But I'm not through with him yet.

Like the well-trained men they are, my two seconds leap into the ring and drag the wimp up, put some fuckin' smelling salts under his nose to revive him, push him again, standing, against the ropes. The guy barely knows where he is. But I'm just getting started. He keeps his fists up like he could fight or something, and I start picking off rights, lefts, small short, sharp jabs that are just enough to wake him up to the pain I'm inflicting. I start banging the guy around the ring and the crowd is wild. Out of the corner of my eye I can see the guys at the back beating off. This is a particularly good slaughter, man, even I know that. My "opponent's" face is a mass of puffy red, and yet he's still standing as I slowly increase the speed and intensity of my leathered fists. I feel each contact with his flesh through my thin fuckin boxing gloves and watch his head flip back with each perfect punch. I muscle him up against the ropes and decide to finish him off like the crowd is screaming for me to do.

One solid left to the face. Fuckin' asshole's right eye closes.

A right to the gut I can feel up to my shoulder. Fuckin' wimp crumples over.

A perfect left, right, left combo that flips the guy up against the ropes again. The guy's fuckin' out on his feet.

But he's still standing.

I don't like that.

I throw a right uppercut like I've never thrown before. The fuckin' asshole's sweat and blood fly, and in slow motion, he starts to sink, his fuckin' beaten, bloody, sweaty body sliding down my front, over my fuckin' raging dick, onto the canvas. Guys in the back groan as they come.

*I groan as I think of what this asshole's mouth will feel
like on my dick when my seconds revive him for round two.*

Jake looked at me warily when I was done, as if antici-
pating disgust. I told him I found it fascinating (even if maybe
he overused *fuckin'*). He sighed with some relief. "You
wouldn't expect it of mild little me, would you? But I tell you,
I caught something in this porno story—when I read it, I feel
like I'm both the guy beating up the kid, and the kid getting
beaten. I don't know what makes it so exciting—except it's so
over-the-top, it's so kind of gory and out there and there's no
moral shit about it. I guess that's what I love about sexual fantasy most—you can escape into it totally, there aren't the
damned *rules* you feel like you have to follow in every other
part of life. And the violence—well, you'll think this is strange,
but I actually don't like most violent movies. I don't even like
suspense movies. The thing about this fantasy is, I get to set the
rules, I get to have it exactly my way. There's something predictable about it, I guess, that makes it 'safe.' You get to do stuff
some deep part of you wants to do—and you can get away with
it. Of course, acting out a fantasy is a different thing. Different
guys I meet are into very specific stuff—one guy gets off on the
boxing gear, another likes to see sweat fly from a punch, another guy just likes uppercuts, another guy just likes body
punches, some guys are into getting marked or bruised, other
guys just want to sort of play at it without throwing real
punches. It's like, in acting out a fantasy, you have to negotiate what portion of your secret world you can let somebody
else into. It often doesn't work. But when it does, there's a feeling of connection that's incredible. Like something really secret is allowed to come out—something you never thought you
could say or share in a million years."

The blood, the violence, savoring inflicting pain on somebody else: these are unnerving aspects of Jake's fantasy even, sometimes, to Jake. "I don't really want to hurt anyone," he says. "But there's something in the fantasy of hurting someone, or getting hurt myself, that's satisfying in a way I can't define. I can figure out some personal reasons for it. I mean, I never rough-housed or anything as a kid. I guess I was your stereotypical well-behaved, repressed, lonely little gay boy. But when I first started to masturbate, whatever was repressed finally had a way to come out—not only in orgasm from my dick, but in my head."

Is this kind of Warrior fantasy "pathology"? We'll examine that question more closely in chapter 4 coming up—but the short answer I'd like to offer here is, "not necessarily." Jake is clear about the difference between having a fantasy and the responsibility you have to another human being acting out that fantasy. "It's been really liberating to me to lose myself in fantasy in my own head—somehow I've never been eaten up by the violence of it. I've just accepted it, the pleasure of it. But even more liberating is being able to find other guys who share some aspects of this fantasy and play it out with each other."

The fact that Jake writes out as well as acts out this fantasy gives a clue about the creative force it's become for him. Writers obsessed by sadomasochism—from the Marquis de Sade through Georges Bataille to the novelist Dennis Cooper (author of such eerie erotica as *Frisk*)—offer in their art what might be seen as a cathartic working through of sadomasochistic fantasy, a kind of closely monitored upwelling from the unconscious into the conscious mind. This transformation can, psychically, be tremendously relieving—even cathartic, curative. In fact, it reflects the express hope and aim of psychoanalysis: Freud once defined the goal of psychoanalysis as bringing the id (the unconscious drives) into the ego (the conscious sense of self). Jake's experiences of articulating, sharing, and getting off on his Warrior fantasies go some way toward achieving this. Releasing fantasy into the conscious mind, and sometimes into conscious action, can constitute a kind of profoundly healing creativity. In his essay "On Narcissism: An Introduction" (S.E., 14:85), Freud quotes a verse by the German romantic poet Heine, about the psychogenesis of creation (*Neue Gedichte*, "Schöpfungslieder VII"), to this effect. God is imagined as saying: "Illness was no doubt the final cause of the whole urge to create. By creating, I could recover; by creating, I became healthy." In the more eloquent German:

> *Krankheit ist wohl der letzte Grund*
> *Des ganzen Schöpferdrangs gewesen;*
> *Erschaffend konnte ich genesen,*
> *Erschaffend wurde ich gesund.*

Jake's Warrior fantasy is, like any fantasy, the product of warring drives and defenses—it constitutes, as does any fantasy, the psyche's attempt to discharge compelling desires that the ego finds threatening: it might thus be seen, in this sense of discomfort, as the kind of illness Heine speaks of. But it is an inevitable discomfort—and finding some way to discharge it is, as Jake has found, a better way of dealing with the discomfort than packing it deeper down and away. More than that, as Heine says God discovered, it is a potentially creative illness when we acknowledge its force and consciously accommodate it—create something from or with it that does justice to the power of the drive. In fact, if we don't find some way to create from these tumultuous forces, we'll be driven by them unconsciously—with a great deal more possibility of danger and self-destruction. The drives, repressed, will not stop operating: indeed, mental illness, a much more destructive affliction than fantasy that can be articulated and consciously acted upon, is the direct result of such repressed drives. Jake has found a channel for something profound in him.

He has learned to give expression to a great column of male Warrior fire: this excites and satisfies him. "I'm calmer, I think, than I would be if I didn't write my pornography and get off on it with other guys. I mean, it's as simple as this: I've built a satisfying outlet for this part of me. It's like physics: if something's held back, it's eventually going to blow up. This is a way of channeling the explosion so that it won't kill me—but it will satisfy me."

However, the explosion remains potentially dangerous—and its power is often horrifying to many of the rest of us who don't feel anywhere near as comfortable as Jake does with acknowledging the brutality of the aggressive urge. Exploring this aspect of ourselves is scary stuff.

Patrick, a determinedly pacifist man in his midforties, first looked at me as if I had two heads when I suggested that sadistic, murderous urges are perfectly normal—and that they existed even in him. "I don't know what all this sadomasochism is about," he said when I told him generally about Jake's fantasy and experiences. "It just leaves me cold. And when you talk about men naturally being 'predators,' I just don't relate. I've only ever desired to have a marriage with someone. To build a home, be faithful, have a dog. I don't even really know what a 'sexual fantasy' *is*. I mean, I don't have elaborate scenarios when I think of sex with my lover. We just touch each other, hold each other, and the rest just happens naturally. The fast-food sex model has never appealed to me: in fact, it disgusts me. It just seems so narcissistic—like using someone else as an object, something to help you masturbate. What does it have to do with making love? If sex isn't gentle, if it doesn't involve caring and trust and warmth—well, it holds no interest for me."

It was true that Patrick had what seemed to be a gentle, old-fashioned relationship with Bill, his lover of seven years. They'd bought a condominium together in suburban Boston and had a wide circle of friends, men and women they worked with or knew from college, some gay, some straight. They traveled together, saved money together, went together to country auctions to buy furniture, had as close to a conventional married life together as any editor of *Family Circle* could envision.

What was bothering Patrick lately didn't, he said, have anything to do with sex. "If there's a problem right now," he said, "it's that I seem to be losing my temper with everyone. It's gotten worse in the past few years. It's like I can't keep myself from sniping at everyone—even Bill. I don't know what's wrong. I like being a teacher [he'd taught high school social studies for ten years], although I'm losing patience with my kids more, too. Bill isn't doing anything wrong—I mean, he's certainly not cheating on me or anything. But sometimes, lately, I can't stand having him in the same room with me. It's like I look at him and some part of me asks, 'Who *is* that guy? What's he doing in my home?' I hate that I feel this way. I feel like something weird is happening inside me, something I can't control. Sometimes I get really depressed over it—it's like some basic dissatisfaction I don't know the source of, and it won't go away." Patrick sighs. "So I've started going to a shrink. I think the weirdest, most upsetting thing about that so far is Bill's reaction. He's thrilled that I'm seeing a therapist. Did I seem to need one that bad? It made me think I don't know how he sees me—how anybody sees me. I'm starting to feel a little . . . I don't know, disembodied, sort of. Like I don't have complete control anymore over how I'm coming across to the world. That's what's scary to me—not anything to do with sex."

When I saw Patrick several months later, I asked him how his therapy was going. His eyes rolled up in his head. "Oh, *God,*" he said. "You don't wanna know." I said, actually I did want to know, if he wanted to tell me. "I almost left the guy," Patrick began. "He kept wanting to talk about my father." I'd known Patrick for years and knew that he hadn't had any contact with his parents since he'd left college. His feelings about his father could be summed up in three words: "I hate him." Patrick groaned again before continuing. "You know how I've cut off relations with my family. Hell, I'd cut them off even when I was living with them, as a kid. My father the Army hero: what could we possibly have had in common? And now, who knows, he's probably some grumbling retired asshole who drinks too much." As unhappy as Patrick was talking about his father, he was less happy about something else: "I've been dreaming about him. Not every night, but at least once a week. It's because of the dreams, which I finally started talking about in therapy, that my shrink is so hot on my tail to talk about my father. And I don't like what's coming up." Patrick laughed, a little grimly. "Come to think of it, though, *you* might like hearing about it. All that aggression you go on about all the time? Well, my father—in my dreams, anyway—is the embodiment of it. They're more nightmares than dreams. The last two were maybe the worst. I never actually *saw* my father in the first of those dreams, but I knew he'd be coming into my bedroom, and I knew he was furious at me. I couldn't think of a reason, I couldn't remember doing anything wrong. But I was paralyzed in bed, and I can't tell you the terror I felt, not knowing when he'd walk through the door, but knowing he would—not knowing what he'd do to me, but knowing it would be terrible."

Patrick eyed me warily. "Don't get any ideas about buried memories of sexual abuse." I assured him I wasn't having any. "Believe me, it's not that. My father never touched me when I was a kid—he never spanked me and he never hugged me. He certainly never molested me. I just didn't exist for him. But what my therapist kept asking me was, what did I think he was going to do to me when he entered my bedroom? I'm not an idiot. I know that whole Freudian idea about dreams being disguised wishes. I knew about transference, too—that by answering that question, I might be saying what I secretly wanted my therapist, my surrogate daddy, to do to me. But I couldn't imagine—I couldn't answer that question. Until, that is, the second dream."

Patrick smiled evilly at me again. "Yeah, you'll like this. The second dream was, I woke up in my childhood bed, opened my eyes to see my father's penis in front of my face. I was fascinated by it. I couldn't imagine what he wanted me to do with it, why it was there. It was long and huge and I finally looked away from it and up into my father's face, and all I could see were his teeth. He was smiling, I could see by the shape of his lips he was smiling, but I could only make out his big white teeth. . . . *Jesus*—you can imagine the field day my shrink had with that one."

Patrick's tone abruptly changed. "But the more important thing is the field day I had with it, I guess. I mean, stuff just poured out of me—all kinds of memories and feelings I didn't know I still had. How much I hated my father. How much—I actually said this—I wanted to *kill* him. This horrible hateful anger in me—God, it was scary how bottomless it seemed to be—it all came raging out. I remembered how, as a little kid, I'd wanted just to get up from our silent dinner table—my little brother and I weren't allowed to talk during dinner—and just scream at my father that I hated him! It was like I'd held back this Tourette's syndrome my whole childhood—all the four-letter words, all the curses, the most horrible invective I could think of—it all boiled up in me now and I started to spit it out at my therapist. At first I made it clear I was feeling it toward my father. But then I started to attack my therapist. How fucking smug he was, listening to me like some goddamn know-it-all. And then Bill—the condescending bastard, what did he really think about me—had he ever in his life been completely honest with me? And then my kids in class—snickering little assholes, probably calling me a queer behind my back. And then you, you with your pontificating about Camille Paglia and the 'uses of sex'—what the hell do *you* know about anything? Who gave you the right to make all these pronouncements? And then that horrible asshole Jake you tell me about who's sick enough to find getting beaten to a pulp a fucking sexual *turn*-on. He's just looking for some fancy psychological excuse for being a fucking *sicko,* and you're playing along to rationalize your own asshole perversions." Patrick paused to catch his breath, his eyes blazing. "It feels like there's fucking *no end* to how much I *hate*—how much I hate every fucking one of you!"

I won't say I enjoyed this recitation—Patrick seemed to realize he'd stepped over some line with me, caught his breath, then spent the next fifteen minutes apologizing for "losing it"—but, on reflection, I saw it as pretty important progress for Patrick. But Patrick came to some sort of realization on his own about the progress this outburst had marked for him. About a week later he called me to say he was feeling better—he apologized again for his outburst—and then paused for a moment, as if considering whether or not he should tell me what was on his mind. "I don't know why," he finally said, "but sex with Bill has become incredible all of a sudden. Maybe there is some connection to all this anger shit about my father—about letting it all rip. I feel freer somehow than I've felt with Bill ever before. What's going on, Mr. Aggression?" I had some ideas, I told him, but I was more interested to hear what he thought was going on. "Beats me," Patrick said. "But someday I'll have to tell you what Bill and I did in bed last night."

Accessing his buried anger was obviously tremendously illuminating, and ultimately therapeutic, to Patrick; he offers an almost unbelievably classic tale about the positive effects of letting out rage. Since this time, we've talked more about my Warrior idea, and it's gotten Patrick to free-associate more about his father. "I don't know about me being a 'warrior,'" he said, "but that dream about my father sticking his dick in my face—well, I realize how erotic it was. I mean, I'm starting to realize that, along with my anger, I'd buried—I guess because I was afraid of it—this real sexual tension between my father and me." Because Patrick was still seeing his shrink, his interest in psychoanalysis had become more acute, and he'd started reading up on Freud's concept of the Oedipus complex. "My father was the 'warrior,' " he said. "I remember all his stories about being in Italy and Germany during the Second World War, all the stuff about his buddies, how he'd seen one of his best friends get blown up right in front of him—when I think of it, that was my main image of him as I grew up. A soldier. But I guess because he seemed to have no use for me, any suggestion of 'soldier' became despicable to me. I mean, hating him meant hating any aggression at all. I know that's too simple. All that stuff about the Oedipus complex, wanting to kill your father and have sex with your mother, and then the castration complex, thinking your father will cut off your dick if you try to take his place—well, I still don't know if I buy all that, but it's made it more vivid not only how much I hated my father, but how afraid I was of him—and how attracted I was to him. Again, I'm not sure if I buy all this, but something in it feels right." The fact that sex with Bill had improved—did he see any clearer reason for that now? "Not really," Patrick said. "I can't come to any easy conclusions about anything. All I know is, I feel freer. And I guess, in a funny way, more of a man. So maybe there is more of a 'warrior' in me than I used to think. But don't count on it."

Patrick's unwillingness to say anything definite about the transition he's undergone is telling: when your psychic bedrock is touched and begins even slightly to shift, it's hard to be clear about what's happening—it's hard to impose any sort of rationale about the shift's sources or ramifications while it's still happening. And particularly when the shift is the result of your confronting long-repressed material—e.g., for Patrick, his anger and fear and sexual feelings about his father—you're going to resist any easy answers. The Oedipus complex is no less horrifying now than it was when Freud first proposed it at the beginning of the century: our taboos against homicidal and incestuous urges against mommy and daddy are terribly forbidding—who would want to face them? We'll have more to say about this in the next section of the book, but right now, it may be sufficient to show that something fierce roils down in the pit of us, which, if we don't acknowledge it, don't find some way to give it expression, will eat away at us like acid. Patrick offers his own experience of tapping that lava and allowing it to erupt: whether or not you or he care to call the new aspect of self that's emerged in him a "warrior" isn't important. What's important is that the lava found some way to shoot out of him.

THE SHAMAN

The mother of all glamour, and therefore of drag, is Medusa, who with her serpent hair, tusks of swine and golden wings, could turn her audience to stone with a look: freezing fear in a glance—every drag queen's dream. To appropriate glamour and desirability to the masculine body against the cultural grain, a gay man has traditionally had to put on the appearance of femininity, the point of which is not to become a woman (they wish to keep their penis) but to bind the fear and fascination of the feminine to the male body.

So writes Mark Simpson in *Male Impersonators: Men Performing Masculinity* (Chapter 9, "Dragging It All Down," p. 178), expressing at a stroke the ambivalent heart of what I identify as the "Shaman" archetype in gay men. "To bind the fear and fascination of the feminine to the male body" describes, I would suggest, not only the drag queen's mission, but to some degree the sexual task and dilemma confronting every gay man.

By fixating on men as sex objects, the most "masculine" gay man has obviously turned one traditional (and, to most heterosexual men, central) notion of masculinity on its ear. In his book *Homos,* Leo Bersani quotes D. A. Miller in Miller's book *Bringing Out Roland Barthes* to this effect: " 'Even the most macho gay image tends to modify cultural fantasy about the male body if only by suspending the main response that the armored body seems developed to induce: if this is still *the body that can fuck you, etc.,* it is no longer—quite the contrary—*the body you don't fuck with.' "* Bersani muses on the gay military man as a kind of nth-degree example of this odd homosexual psychic mixture: "In imagining what he presumably already is (both gay and Marine), the gay Marine may learn the invaluable lesson that *identity is not serious* (as if what he is imitating never existed before it was imitated)."

It is a premise of this book that gay male identity *is,* in a sense, "serious": the masculine and feminine drives that impel us seem to me too overwhelmingly strong to be entirely learned from culture and family. I'm uncomfortable with entirely relativistic premises about gender, which is why I've invoked Camille Paglia and her male/female dichotomies that rage with such biological inevitability and power. There does seem, finally, something torrentially, almost hormonally, given about the Warrior fire in us; equally so about what I call the Shaman impulse. But Simpson, Bersani, et al. do illuminate what ultimately I see as gay men's extraordinary ability to play with various elements of their identity, however escapable or inescapable they may be. Identity can, after all, be "serious" *and* playful. The divided men we've already met give ample evidence of this (e.g., Jake's mild-mannered public persona and his private raging, fighting sexual self). Heterosexual men do seem to cling desperately to what is finally a shallow myth—that "real men" don't (or shouldn't) have these kinds of splits: they must be armored with "masculinity" every breathing moment of their lives. However, we, to their horror, are "the body that fucks" *and* "the body you fuck with." That second part of our identity opens enormous realms for us against which straight men defend themselves with a desperate, perhaps even poignant, vengeance.

However, "the body you fuck with" implies a passivity that I would not ascribe to my Shaman archetype. A better phrase might be "the body *I let* you fuck with." The goddess roots of the Shaman are far from passive, benign, or pretty. They are chaotically powerful and dangerous—in direct opposition to the clear, hard-edged beauty of Apollo. In *Sexual Personae*, Camille Paglia speaks of the "chthonian" nature of the fecund, fetid Dionysian realm—*chthonian* meaning "of the earth":

> . . . but earth's bowels, not its surface. . . . The Dionysian is no picnic. It is the chthonian realities which Apollo evades, the blind grinding of subterranean force, the long slow suck, the murk and ooze. It is the dehumanizing brutality of biology and geology, the Darwinian waste and bloodshed, the squalor and rot we must block from consciousness to retain our Apollonian integrity as persons. Western science and aesthetics are attempts to revise this horror into imaginatively palatable form.
>
> The daemonism of chthonian nature is the west's dirty secret. (pp. 5, 6)

The "daemonism of chthonian nature" is also the "dirty secret" of sex, perhaps more dramatically present in gay men than in anyone else because of the extreme tension in each of us between Apollo and Dionysus. The beauty and glamour of the drag queen, the sexual fusion in the shaman, are an intensely keyed-up expression of this tension—although even they are to a degree Apollo-ized, cleaned-up, more aesthetic versions of a great dark sucking mystery, a mystery Paglia finds archetypically "female." But we still sense a primal, fatal danger at the heart of even this "cleaned-up" mystery; the world of the Shaman, of the drag queen, and (I would argue) of every sexual gay man is the underworld: it is a world of bursting, dark fullness. Paglia makes this vivid as she speaks of "Teiresias, the androgynous Greek shaman," "depicted as an old man with long beard and pendulous female breasts. . . . It is as if Teiresias, in the underworld of racial memory, represents a fullness of emotional knowledge fusing sexes" (p. 45).

Go to Cherry Grove on Fire Island and look at the challenging, provocative beauty of the drag queen for a real, here-on-earth strong dose of divine goddess-glamour; "she" is "chthonian" power wonderfully gussied up, with the power, as Mark Simpson says of Medusa, to "turn her audience to stone with a look: freezing fear in a glance." But this female goddess "knowledge" isn't limited to drag queens; as I've proposed, it exists in all of the rest of us, too—no less than the arcing supermale Apollo: we are creatures who embody both impulses more completely and excitingly than most heterosexuals ever could, because it is stained into our sexual selves, lives, experience, more indelibly: we fuck *and* get fucked.

Just as Jake liked thinking of himself as a "warrior," Alan, a thirty-eight-year-old Episcopal priest, has come to understand his own "Shaman" nature. "That's exactly the right word for what's been most liberating to me about finally accepting my sexuality—hell, accepting that I'm sexual," Alan says. "I sometimes used to think of what pulled me into the priesthood in psychoanalytic terms: looking for an omnipotent father who would take care of me in some ultimate way. But lately I've been seeing that pull differently. I had what amounts to a huge crisis of faith—I got to the point where I wanted to take out a machine gun and spray bullets into the front pew at all the smug, falsely pious blue-haired ladies who stared up at me every Sunday while I preached my sermons. My sermons were getting more and more iconoclastic, at least in the eyes of these conservatives—I was preaching Christ's message of life and joy in ways that embraced the physical, the sexual, the material appetites with which every human being is endowed. I found myself again and again calling for us to take risks—to seek full, sensual pleasure in every aspect of life, including sex. My ladies looked increasingly bewildered: they couldn't relate. I saw that I was really giving voice to my own frustration about the lack of pleasure in my life, sort of taking it out on whoever sat in front of me in church. I was angry, angry at the complacent ruts so many people make of church and religion. But really I was angry at myself."

Alan grew up, he said, "as close to asexual as it is possible to be. Not only asexual, but afraid to let myself go physically in any way. I actually cried a while back when I watched, for the first time in about fifteen years, some home movies my parents had put onto a VHS tape as a birthday present." Alan snorts. "What a bomb of a present—it devastated me. There was me as a two-year-old, wobbling along, obviously trying to get my parents' attention, hopping like a duck when we are at the zoo, smiling and chattering and so anxious to get someone to look at me. That voracious hunger to be seen—it was so naked I could hardly look at it. Then, at about six or seven, something in me seemed to shut down. I looked so tentative, so cautious, in every shot—every step, every gesture was so careful, delicate, effeminate. I looked like a little girl afraid to get her Sunday clothes dirty. It was really hard to look at myself; I felt such shame about this delicate, painfully self-conscious, girlish boy. But worse was a brief moment—it didn't last longer than maybe five seconds—of me at twelve, on a family vacation to Chicago, running wildly, like some spastic scarecrow, across a busy street. It was the only moment caught on film of me really letting go—and I was obviously so *bad* at it, I mean, so clumsy and unused to just running for the hell of it. For that tiny five-second period, some little burst of energy was allowed to explode out of me, and it was heartbreaking to me to see how unfamiliar the burst obviously was. Every other moment in the film, right up to my college graduation and ordination as a priest, was that hemmed-in, overcautious, anxious-to-please little boy again. I'd never seen so vividly before how trapped I was."

Shortly after he got this "bomb of a present," Alan was invited to what he knew was going to be an outrageous Halloween party. "I was apprehensive about going at first—I knew this was going to be a screamingly 'gay' party and I'd never been comfortable with that kind of in-your-face bitchy gay stuff. I'd come out in seminary—probably because so many other aspiring Episcopal priests were such queens, there didn't seem to be any reason not to come out. I've said I was asexual, and that's true—I'd successfully blocked erotic feelings about anyone, male or female, throughout all of my adolescence. I'd get emotional crushes on various boys and teachers, but the sexual part of me was so dammed off that it never occurred to me I could be sexual with any of them. Literally the only time I reached orgasm was via wet dreams. The fantasies that made me come were really vague, not really involving any actual human being—they were more a kind of purely physical thing, like me rubbing against my sheets or my pillow." Alan laughs. "In fact, if I had any erotic object at all, it was probably my bed."

But by the time of the Halloween party, Alan had been living with a "roommate/sort-of-lover for several years. We played around more than had out-and-out satisfying sex. What one seminarian friend of mine called 'the Princeton rub,' what others call frottage: we'd sort of writhe against each other in the dark until we came. It feels to me now, looking back, like a kind of proto-sex—something that just happened, not something we put a lot of energy into, planned for, or got excited about. I'd never really had sexual fantasies per se—I didn't even find gay pornography especially exciting. Actually, I found it frightening. Big-dicked porno stars seemed like an entirely different species from me. I couldn't imagine actually touching one—much less having sex with one. They were from some totally different world, a world that had nothing to do with me."

And yet Alan had for some time been on his "sermon rampage about enjoying our God-given appetites I've already told you about. Even though my own sex life was pretty tepid, some frustration was really mounting in me—it fueled the call for pleasure I kept haranguing my blue-haired ladies with—something pent up in me obviously wanted to be released." Alan smiles suddenly, mischievously: "That Halloween party was, to put it mildly, the occasion for it."

It was a costume party given, Alan says, "by the only outrageous gay couple my partner and I knew, two men in their fifties, Andy and Thomas, who'd lived together for twenty years, bragged incessantly about the young boys they somehow succeeded in luring up to their apartment to have sex with—sort of stereotypical old-time queers, I guess—caftans, opera, Judy Garland, crystal chandeliers, the whole bit. 'Honey,' Andy said when he invited me to the party, 'you'd better dress up for this one. I'm not letting you in the door unless you look very, very *gay*.' "

Alan pauses for a moment. "I came as a nun." He laughs. "I can't tell you what a hoot it was. I also don't know where I got the courage to do it—I mean, I'd never been in drag before in my life. And this wasn't just any old nun. I actually drummed up the nerve to buy up the Revlon counter at Macy's—I was one *made-up* sister, I can tell you. Jeff, my partner, couldn't believe what I looked like—he chickened out himself and came as a sort of watered-down pirate (basically wore a hat, eye patch, and vest)—he just kept staring at me. He said what was really weird was how *beautiful* I looked. 'I never knew you had such incredibly beautiful eyes!' Eye makeup can do some amazing stuff."

Even weirder, to Alan, was the "persona that got unleashed at the party. I was there in my flowing robes, made up like Mamie Van Doren playing the Flying Nun, and I suddenly got outrageous—of course I drank quite a bit, too, which helped. It was like there was this full-blown queen who finally got the chance to strut out and wow the crowd. I was bitchy, funny, seductive—sashaying around the room, feeling up various men's asses and crotches: where the hell did *this* all come from? It was an absolute revelation. It felt so completely natural—it was as if I'd unleashed some graceful she-devil who'd existed in me completely formed and ready to rip."

When Alan and Jeff got home—"we were the last to leave the party"—"the outrageousness," Alan said, "was still in full bloom. I was also still pretty high, which partly accounts for all this, but when we walked into the house, I grabbed Jeff's hand, pulled him into the bedroom—still in full nun drag, of course—and pulled Jeff onto the bed. 'Fuck me,' I curtly directed him. Jeff, eye patch still in place, was astonished. But, well, right there, pulling up my black skirts and pulling down my underwear, pulling down his pants and producing a packet of lube and a condom from God knew where—he complied." Alan sighed. "It felt like the first sex I'd ever had in my life. In a way, I guess it *was* the first sex I'd ever had."

The most unexpected dividend from releasing what Alan calls "the bitch goddess me" hasn't been his new capacity to enjoy sex: "it's what it's done to me spiritually. I think I always saw the church before as something to escape into, something that would take over my life and make my decisions for me, allowing me some way to avoid becoming a fully functioning, physical, sexual human being. I could just dump all my anxieties and energies into God's lap—let Him take care of it. But it's like God stood up and dumped all that stuff back out of his lap onto me. I actually fantasized God as saying, 'This isn't my stuff, it's yours. Deal with it.' That 'stuff' has turned out to be the backed-up sensual me—the reason the five-second home-movie moment of me, at twelve, maniacally laughing and running goofily across the street, struck me to my very soul was that I'd come face-to-face with what was missing in my life now: *joy*. The joy I kept going on about in my sermons. Now, when I face my blue-haired ladies, I see them with more compassion. I've connected more with my *mission*, I guess, the thing that spiritually and unconsciously must really have drawn me to the priesthood—the reason I'm a priest, which is *not* just some neurotic Oedipal need for a Big Daddy in the Sky. My mission as a priest really *is* what I think of as the mission of a Shaman: someone who's able to bring the physical and the spiritual together in his own life, not just orate about it. Any power I have to touch other people's souls comes from the experience of having allowed my own soul to be touched—hell, more than touched: fucked. The bitch goddess has met the frightened, spiritually and emotionally constipated child I once was and told him he could have what he really desperately, secretly wanted to have all along: a hell of a good time. It's no wonder 'Auntie Mame' has such power for us. The thing is, I don't have to look elsewhere for Mame: she resides, in full outrageous splendor, right in the center of me." Alan cocks his head and bats his eyelashes: "Of course in *me* she's more like Mamie Van Doren."

ROLE-PLAYING AS REVOLUTION

I had an experience—and awakening—somewhat similar to Alan's about ten years ago in Cherry Grove, Fire Island. My then lover and I were invited to a party at which costumes of one sort or another were de rigueur. Apart from a few mostly blocked-out memories of my childhood where I sneaked into my mother's closet and put on one of her slips—or mincingly ran, unobserved (I hoped), as a seven-year-old along an uninhabited stretch of South Shore Long Island beach trailing a huge beach towel like a princess's train—I had had no experience of drag; in fact, I had a sort of horror of it. I was uncomfortable talking to the magnificent ladies of Cherry Grove. I felt as if they *were* frightening Medusas, who, on a whim, with the bat of a two-inch eyelash, could very well have turned me to stone. When I think of it, I was as scared of them as I ever was of any intimidating junior-high macho bully: they expressed some extreme of which I thought myself incapable.

But I dressed up for *this* party, and it was amazing. I borrowed a platinum blond wig, sheer, glittery stockings, and man-sized, red fuck-me pumps from an obliging "Medusa" who lived in our house. I slipped a Day-Glo floral bikini bottom over the stockings, which shockingly outlined and pumped up the bulge in my crotch, then topped all this off with a butch red satin baseball jacket, opened to show off my hairy chest, and a hot pink feather boa. A touch of blazing red lipstick gleamed out from my full beard: I was complete.

I was hardly a standout at the party; most men looked far more fabulous than I did. But I somehow nonetheless caught the eye of a photographer from the *Fire Island Times* and ended up on the centerfold of the following week's paper: my first time in semidrag did *not,* in other words, go unpublicized. But my most vivid memory of the bitch goddess me was walking back from the party—tediously slowly, awestruck by others who seemed to be able to tromp in spike heels without breaking their legs on the boardwalk—and a drunken young partygoer from some other house stopping in his tracks at the sight of me, then marching up to me and kissing me hard on the mouth, cupping my crotch with both hands. *"God,* you're hot," he said. Hot? I was a walking gargoyle—at least in my own mind's eye. But it was thrilling, not to say flattering, to feel the sexuality of the bitch goddess, not just her outrageous absurdity. It made it clear to me that I hadn't, as some people say when they opine about drag queens, "found the woman in me." I had found the drag queen in me. The goddess, the bitch, the sexually fused Shaman. I still felt very male—but there was lipstick next to my beard. Something in me had expanded to include not a female energy, but a peculiarly *homosexual* energy.

There is something essentially playful and ironic about this energy. As Mark Simpson says (again in *Male Impersonators,* p. 179): "For all its possible denigration of the feminine body, drag has the effect, unwitting or not, of pointing up the foolishness of gender *performance;* by putting a man in a frock, gender itself is *de*frocked and put in the stocks for a day." The sexual roles we play never lack this irony—we are always, in some sense, putting on a performance of something iconographic. The icons, among them the Warrior and the Shaman, have tremendous power; I would once again maintain that they are rooted in the most primal sources of self. But when we become conscious of them as icons, we can begin to turn them to our own uses and will. We start to gain some power over our volcanic eruptions; we don't merely react when we're unconsciously hit upside the head by one or another force we've dangerously repressed.

A profound freedom of self can result from this consciousness, this growing ability to make *use* of the archetypes that rage up within us. We can never banish the power, and the danger, of the source of these forces, but it is possible to learn to ride them—surf the unconscious, if you will—without falling off and killing ourselves. Because the divided forces in gay men are so urgent, so compelling, we have an extraordinary opportunity to expand the sense of what's possible, what's allowable, in the expression of these forces. We have no choice but to accommodate our sexual and psychic volcanoes: they will erupt whether or not we want them to. But we do, at least potentially, have the choice to become conscious of them—even to have fun with them.

This constitutes what is for me a dual sense of revolution: the first, a revolution in the usual political sense, the abrupt and liberating eruption of a new and wider self-affirmation, a new and wider repertory of roles and states of being that change how we interact with others in the world—and thus stand to change that world itself, by changing its perceptions of us. But I also mean revolution in a more literal sense: the personal ability to revolve from one state of being to another, the ability to be both shaman and warrior—to be Clark Kent, Superman, and Lois Lane: to *move* between and among these different selves without feeling shame that we're not (as we may think we have to be) Superman, or any other singular homogeneous self, every moment of our lives. The ability to create beauty in and out of chthonian darkness in a million different ways; to judge none of those creations automatically as sick, to celebrate the ones we can celebrate: this is what leads to freedom, and not solely sexual freedom.

Of course, this is nothing but stirring rhetoric unless we're able to stumble onto the kinds of receptivity we've seen in every man so far in this book: a theme common to all of them might be summed up as courage—the courage to look at moments of self-exposure, moments of vulnerability and shame, without bolting away. We are always revealing ourselves: the unconscious might be seen as attempting continually to flag the conscious mind down. *"This* is what I want, *this* is what I need, damn you: can't you see?" Our ids are screaming babies and they will not let up. So much of what we've learned to do in the face of this eternal screaming need is to find ways to block out the scream—to pretend we're not the hungry, howling infants we really are. The cost of this pretense is enormous: ultimately it can kill us. When a volcano can't explode, it implodes—and that can wreak a terribly self-destructive havoc.

Turning these inner forces outward—giving the unconscious conscious expression—is something we'll explore more fully in the next section of this book. We've seen how traditional notions of masculinity and femininity can profitably be turned on their respective ears: now it's time to do the same thing to notions of pathology. At what (if any) point do our sexual self-views, fantasies, and behavior become sick? Is it right to be a complete relativist about this? (Can we really condone Jake for getting a hard-on over the idea of being beaten to a pulp?)

The gay men you'll soon meet have grappled with these questions in some compelling ways, which may illuminate what's really being asked in those questions more fully than you expect.

FOUR

OUR
OWN
PRIVATE
IDAHOS

**REASSESSING
SEXUAL PATHOLOGY,
COMPULSION, AND
DYSFUNCTION**

THE CLASSICAL FREUDIAN PSYCHOAN-
alytical view of human maturation might be likened to a trip on the Long Island Rail Road from Montauk to Manhattan. You're born in Montauk, experience the infant oral, anal, and phallic stages as you trundle through East, South, and West Hampton, hit the Oedipal stage around Sayville, change trains at Babylon for latency, the thick of which you're into by Massapequa Park (yo—Joey Buttafuoco!), struggle through adolescence all the way to bleak Jamaica, and finally, sweaty and tired and battle-worn, achieve "mature" heterosexuality by the time you get to Penn Station (for old age, take the Path train to Newark?). It's an exhausting trip, with any number of storm warnings, track changes, equipment breakdowns en route—and

woe be to you if you get off at Massapequa Park (and get stuck, as homosexuals are thought by this model to do, in the latency stage).

This idea of heterosexuality being the jackpot of human maturation has passed into our consciousness like a serum injected into us in infancy: it is part of the Western zeitgeist, an unquestioned manifest-destiny view of the normal human psyche. The implicit assumptions of pathology it engenders are subtle and crippling—and seductive to the point of seeming, sometimes, inarguable.

In fact, the more I am exposed to psychoanalytic attempts to codify or explain human behavior, the more aware (and wary) I become of the seductions of thinking psychoanalytically. In the psychoanalytic zeal to ferret out and define the sources of human behavior, it seems to me that we often seek what amounts to a dismissal of human behavior—to tie it up, label it—put it, in effect, out of mind where it won't bother us anymore. But there may be a way to find more generative ideas in psychoanalytic theory, not by taking what it tells us as foregone truth, but rather looking at its assumptions and deductions more speculatively, metaphorically—with some of the same limits but also the same potential illumination as Camille Paglia's extrapolations from Apollo and Dionysus.

I've tried to keep theory to a minimum in this book: it seems far more productive to examine the details of actual gay men's experience than to quote and argue with theoreticians, except as they momentarily add juice or perspective to whatever aspect of real gay male experience we're looking at. The aim in these pages is frankly therapeutic: it amounts to calling for us to find ways to liberate our erotic lives and imaginations. Others have navigated the ocean of psychoanalytic misapprehensions regarding homosexuality more widely and deeply than I am equipped to do: e.g., the aforementioned Simpson and Bersani, and of course Michel Foucault, among numerous others (see the bibliography for a sampling). But because the assumption of pathology is still so rampant in even many gay men's approach to much of gay male sex, we will at least put our toes into the water here.

We'll start by taking on (variously agreeing and arguing with) what I think are helpful psychoanalytic ideas and formulations from two current neo-Freudian analysts, Christopher Bollas (in his book *Being a Character: Psychoanalysis and Self Experience*) and Joyce McDougall (in *The Many Faces of Eros: A Psychoanalytic Exploration of Human Sexuality*). I've chosen Bollas and McDougall because in my own reading in psychoanalysis I stumbled onto their intensely interesting psychoanalytic work—work that embraces the drives I hold to be so important in the ways we perceive and act out our sexual lives. They are (in their incorporation of Freudian drive theory) unapologetic children of Freud; hence my appellation "neo-Freudian." But they use Freud in wonderfully imaginative, generative ways. They might each be thought of as liberal psychoanalysts—psychoanalysts who in a debate with Jesse Helms would come down solidly on our side. This makes some of their assumptions about gay male pathology all the more sorely evident; they don't always *apply* their generative models as completely, profitably, or imaginatively as they might to gay men and sex. However, Bollas depatricizes the Oedipal drama in ways that I think speak directly to our gay male experience; McDougall explores evidence that we choose our sexual objects as attempts at self-cure, an idea which I think has fascinating, healing implications.

"GENERATIVE ASYLUMS": RETHINKING PATHOLOGY WITH CHRISTOPHER BOLLAS

Christopher Bollas, a member of the British Psycho-Analytical Society and book review editor of the *International Journal of Psychoanalysis,* is appealing to me partly because he writes so damned well, but even more because he widens the idea of what the Oedipal complex is. We don't necessarily end up in Penn Station at the end of his version of the Oedipal drama: we may well end up jumping off the train (at or after Sayville) and hitchhiking to Idaho. But getting to Idaho (or wherever else we may want to end up) is no less fraught with danger. Bollas's genuine attempts to keep the Oedipal field open are potentially as much an invitation to madness and despair as to any kind of psychic, maturational freedom. Indeed, the "Why Oedipus?" chapter of *Being a Character* takes us right to the brink. In Bollas's provocative rereading of Oedipus and its Freudian applications, he expresses a much less patriarchal view of the Oedipal child's crisis than Freud offered: instead of necessarily fighting the father for the mother's love, the Oedipal child (boy or girl) "realizes in quite a profound way that the father preceded the child's relation to the mother, and it is the recognition of such precedents—on the part of both girl and boy—that is an identification: a correct identification of one's place, of one's position in time." The child's "anguish in the triangle is resolved to the point of a form of liberation from it—a liberation from dilemma into complexity" (pp. 230, 231).

Bollas develops the idea of the child not having an Oedipus complex but *being* one—that the "Oedipal child's moment of truth" is realizing the " 'itness' of his own mind . . . that painful but gradual recognition in the child that the dream he dreams is

not an event external to the self that awakening or parental sooth-
ing can dispel, but an internal event entirely sponsored by the
child's own mind"—he constructs a sense of recognizing one's
own complexity and isolation, which is as potentially shattering
as liberating. He says we survive the terrifying recognition of our
essential aloneness by "devolution," a regression back to dyadic
(e.g., you and mommy) and triadic states (e.g., you, mommy, and
daddy) in which we re-create pre-Oedipal comforts with best
friends, lovers, spouses, and families. In other words, we survive
by learning to create and go back to a fictive innocence, to pretend that close relationships can give us the safety we once
yearned for pre-Oedipally from our parents. To survive (and to
position ourselves so that we might feel some pleasure in living),
we opt for a kind of selective blindness or denial; we must deny
a central, devastating reality, which is simply that we are each of
us unutterably, and to some degree unreachably, separate—alone.

In these survival-motivated regressions, we also, Bollas says,
"retreat . . . forward into passionate beliefs in the veracity of a single vision of reality (whether a psychoanalytic view, a political
opinion, or a theological perspective), all unconsciously sooth-
ing—even when the occasions of mental pain themselves—
because the mentally objectifiable dilemma is always preferable
to the complex that is beyond its mental processing." So the child-
as-Oedipal complex, conscious that he is himself a complex, allows himself what amounts to only a fleeting exposure to the true
nature of reality (his unknowable and complex singularity) before he retreats to the survival tactics of play—creating for himself a world that at least has the illusion of comfort. "Knowing
this"—what Bollas calls "the solitude of subjectivity"—"life becomes an effort to find inner sanctuary from the logic of psy-
chodevelopment, and when this generative asylum is established
it allows the subject to play with the samples of reality that pass
by him during his lifetime."

This is what I find liberating—Bollas's idea of the "generative asylum," that in the necessary fictions we must tell ourselves to survive, we develop the same creative capacities we've seen throughout the stories of men in this book: we learn to create our own freedom. Unfortunately, Bollas does not pursue this idea where I think it most needs to be pursued—in reflections on various aspects of gay male sex that he offers in his essay "Cruising in the Homosexual Arena." Questioning various assumptions about pathology that he seems to me to make will help us, I think, to question similar assumptions in ourselves.

I began by stating my wariness about what psychoanalytic thinking can devolve into—a dismissal of human reality, rather than a means of truly apprehending it (which, by Bollas's lights, we can be forgiven for not wanting to do, so complex and horrifying is this reality). The most convenient way of dismissing human behavior is to apply a model of pathology to it. And, with Freudian ammunition, there is no end to the pathology we can find. Indeed, any choice we make, because it involves the renunciation of other choices, which creates conflict and frustration, is virtually by definition "neurotic"—a kind of pathology.

Nowhere has the pathological model been more reflexively applied than to homosexuality. The suspension of judgment, the wide-ranging and curious "playful" exploration of human motive that I find elsewhere in Christopher Bollas's writing, I find less of in his piece about gay cruising. As many disclaimers as he gives about gay men and the "sexual arena," that this arena can for some gay men represent an important self-exploration and self-affirmation, he still creates for me an unnecessarily pathological model for the gay man engaged in anonymous sex. Bollas is, as usual, a wonderful writer and often brilliantly evocative about the experience of men who are troubled by their sexual behavior (he admits that these troubled men are the gay men he knows best, and that this is a limitation), but finally I don't see that the various models he proposes for how gay men express themselves sexually are any more pathological or maladaptive than the way any adult sexual being works out his or her expression of sexuality. There is, it seems to me, a kind of cultural bias in Christopher Bollas's thinking that has limited if not distorted it.

Basically Bollas's point about gay men who frequent the anonymous sex arenas of parks, discos, and baths is that frequently these men, as children, experience an "anguish" that "emerges from some perhaps hidden break with the parents. This break is a terrible loss of the parenting skills needed by a child growing up in the world; this child cannot be the parent's boy, and is unsure if he can become his own person. In my view, as he experiences this loss, he often loses the authorizing force of his true self and projects its strength into an ideal alter self. As he cannot maintain his personal strength in the face of blocks to his evolution, he projects it into an ideal boy that may later in adult life be adored back into reality. Love of the boy or the ideal body is a reclamatory love, an effort to unite with the divided half, to overcome one's deficiency and isolation. Needless to say, this alter being that possesses lost parts of the self is the object of intense need, the objectification of anguishing loss and, when it is acted out with the other, of a most ironic envy and hate."

Most of this discussion of "reclamatory love," the "effort to unite with the divided half, to overcome one's deficiency and isolation," strikes me as a reasonably good generic description of *any* human being's motive, particularly in light of Bollas's existentially terrifying Oedipal moment, which, according to him, plunges us into a devastating sense of our aloneness—which we'll do anything to escape. This "deficiency" of self is one, it seems to me, that is felt by every post-Oedipal (in Bollas's sense of Oedipal) human being, straight or gay. The search for an "alter being" is not one limited to gay men cruising the sexual arena: this being is every bit as desperately searched for by the average un-married heterosexual small-town lady librarian. Furthermore, his sense of an "alter being that possesses lost parts of the self" and "is the object of intense need, the objectification of anguishing loss and, when it is acted out with the other, of a most ironic envy and hate" again describes the unconscious needs, desires, feelings, and fantasies of any person who is sexually aroused by or in love with any other person—up to and including "a most ironic envy and hate." Welcome to human relationships, not just gay men having anonymous sex.

I don't mean to gloss over the differences: I am not saying that a small-town lady librarian dreaming of marriage and a white picket fence and a gay man cruising for sex in the local bus-station men's room are (necessarily) after the same things. I would, how-ever, suggest that we not automatically apply the pathological label to the gay man (or, for that matter, to the lady librarian). But neither am I claiming that the kind of anonymous sex to which Bollas devotes himself in this piece is not sometimes an acting out of despair; of course it is—maybe it even often is. However, the process of "sexual execution" that Bollas ascribes to these gay men points out a basic, inescapable truth about any sexual encounter. We commonly objectify each other into some state of romantic or sexual itness—again, it is Bollas who tells us (in "Why Oedipus?") we resort to various forms of selectively blind objectification/falsification to survive (and certainly to have sex: what human being comes to orgasm without some form of this objectification?). "Out of the shadows of a park, a bar, or a cinema, anonymous others casually embody the transient nature of the psychic world, meeting up in an intermediate space where actual self and the internal object-rival encounter one another." Yeah—sounds like what happens at the average senior prom or office Christmas party to me. This "intermediate space" is the space inhabited by any two people in a state of sexual tension.

Bollas evocatively quotes a number of gay novelists (John Rechy, James Baldwin, Andrew Holleran) about the deadening effect of so much anonymous cruising and sex. He speaks of John Rechy's sense of "arena": "the gay place for some homosexuals is, as Rechy calls it, an 'arena' for the gathering of deadened selves looking for some erotic salvation for their plight." This seems to make his sense and description of the plight of gay men inarguable: from their own ranks, gay men—these novelists—bemoan the objectification and emptiness of casual, anonymous sex. But these are novelists, writing evocative fiction, not irrefutable truths about the whole range of gay male sexual behavior and attitudes. The plight of gay men is by no means sewn up by these fictions, however evocative of and even truthful about some gay male experiences they may be.

Of course anonymous sex can bespeak the kind of pathology—the kind of emptiness and objectification—Bollas explores here. But it doesn't have to be seen this way. It's not that as gay men we haven't battled low self-esteem. It's not that we don't struggle with intimacy or how to live with each other as lovers and friends, how to have mature romantic relationships. (Who doesn't?) But, as this book has already gone some distance in demonstrating, there is something else alive, important, and compelling going on, too, something gay men haven't sufficiently publically acknowledged: the secret truths, deeper connections, the intimacies, the wisdom, the darkness and the light, despair and elation, boredom and breakthroughs of this superabundance of sex so many of us can't seem to stop thinking about or having. In other words, anonymous and/or kinky sex for gay men can be seen as an expression of life (however bound up with Paglia's chthonian darkness), not necessarily pathology—a peculiar expression of how we deal with that complex and devastating post-Oedipal reality Christopher Bollas describes so vividly.

I'll go further: it is normal for us to want to have a lot of sex, to experience conflict and terror and both illuminating and unnerving discoveries in the mental and physical pursuit of sex. It is normal to be disturbed by the urgency of this search. It is normal for the search never to end. Our sexual lives define something precious and interesting about who we are. We don't need to apologize for them; we can benefit, rather, from acknowledging their complex reality (and pleasure and danger and devastation and boredom), at least to ourselves—and then, with as full a consciousness as we can muster, *play* with what we find, enjoy it to whatever edge we feel we can bring it without doing ourselves in.

I'm aware that all of the above can be attacked psychoanalytically—that this sort of Jungian-sounding archetypal talk is all very stirring, but we still have Christopher Bollas's patients, and their complaints, and his (no doubt) accurate analysis of those complaints. I would just ask him—and us—to see the gay male experience more expansively, more in light of his own wonderfully frightening and encompassing sense of human reality that he talks about so beautifully elsewhere in his work—especially in "Why Oedipus?"

THE NORMALITY OF TRAUMA, SYMPTOMS AS SELF-CURE: LEARNING FROM JOYCE McDOUGALL

Joyce McDougall, a training and supervising analyst at the Paris Psychoanalytical Society, offers in her recent book, *The Many Faces of Eros,* a magnificent opening sentence, one that in many ways sums up the premise of these pages: "Human sexuality," she writes, "is inherently traumatic." She explains:

> *The many psychic conflicts encountered in the search*
> *for love and satisfaction, arising as a result of the clash be-*
> *tween the inner world of primitive instinctual drives and the*
> *constraining forces of the external world, begin with our first*
> *sensuous relationship. When the baby encounters the*
> *"breast-universe," the period of "cannibal love," in which*
> *erotic and sadistic strivings are conflated, is inaugurated.*
> *The slowly acquired notion of an "other"—of an object sep-*
> *arate from the self—is born out of frustration, rage, and a*
> *primitive form of depression that every baby experiences in*
> *relation to the primordial object of love and desire. Felicity*
> *lies in the abolition of the difference between the self and*
> *other. (P. ix)*

The stage is thus set for Christopher Bollas's frightening "solitude of subjectivity": all of us, as infants, profoundly resist the notion that we are separate from the flesh and presence of the mother, often (quite literally) kicking and screaming against this growing realization of our apartness, until that fleeting Oedipal moment where, as Bollas tells us, we encounter the full horrifying realization of our own "itness"—and then flee it by any possible means.

These means make themselves known frequently as "symptoms": we do not hate or love, deny or obsess about various elements in our psyches and external worlds arbitrarily: hates and loves serve the psyche's very specific continuing attempts to ward off what it perceives as dire threats, and to draw to itself what it perceives as necessary to its survival. McDougall neatly states another premise that proceeds from this idea, which I also hold:

> *Psychological symptoms are attempts at self-cure, to*
> *avoid psychic suffering; the same intent applies equally to*
> *symptomatic sexuality. Taking this more constructive view*

> *of the underlying meaning and purpose of symptoms, and*
> *the reasons for which they came into being, we invariably*
> *discover that they are childlike solutions to conflict, confu-*
> *sion, and mental pain. Faced with the difficulties of being*
> *human, as well as the unconscious conflicts of our parents,*
> *we must all contrive ways of surviving, both as individuals*
> *and as sexual beings, and the solutions we find tend to en-*
> *dure for a lifetime. (p. 172)*

The ways in which we manifest our sexuality have a life-or-death force and urgency. We cannot lightly abandon these sexual "symptoms" because of our own or anyone else's disapprobation of them. As McDougall says, ". . . to lose one's only system of sexual survival would be the equivalent of castration. And more than that. In many cases, these intricate and ineluctable erotic scenarios serve not only to safeguard the feeling of sexual identity that accompanies sexual pleasure, but frequently reveal themselves to be techniques of psychic survival that are required to preserve the feeling of subjective identity as well."

McDougall has coined the term "neosexualities" to describe various versions of "deviant" hetero- and homo-sexual*ities* ("[t]he variations in psychosexual structure are so great that we are obliged to talk in the plural"), which often "require fetishistic additions, such as shoes or whips, or sadomasochistic conditions of pain or humiliation, in order to achieve satisfactory sexual engagement." While she does not consider homosexuality a "neosexuality," she does suggest that "the one area that is characteristic of both homosexual and neosexual patients concerns the psychic economy that governs their sexuality. This economy is frequently marked by a sense of urgency and compulsivity, giving the impression that their sexual lives fulfill the role of an addiction." (p. 175)

McDougall's emphasis on symptoms as attempts at self-cure is not new, but she makes it with resounding force, and this assertion strikes me as one of the most potentially liberating ideas gay men can consider about their own sexual universes. She is to be lauded for standing back from making easy judgments. When she grapples with what may or may not be "perverse" sexual fantasy, McDougall says: "In my view the only aspect of a fantasy that might legitimately be described as perverse would be the attempt to force one's erotic imagination on a non-consenting or a non-responsible other" (p. 177). Simply because we may find one or another sexual practice personally objectionable does not allow us to confer upon it any judgment of pathology: "The quality of a relationship cannot be assessed from purely external signs. There are qualitative as well as quantitative psychic factors to be taken into account. . . . Human sexual patterns, as Freud was the first to point out, are not inborn; they are created" (p. 178).

As to the choice we feel about the sexual scenarios or objects that obsess us—well, we don't have much. "Nobody freely *chooses* to engage in the highly restricted and exigent conditions imposed by compulsive neosexual inventions," McDougall says:

> *With regard to deviant heterosexual, homosexual, and autoerotic inventions, these so-called choices represent the best possible* solutions *created by the child of the past in the face of contradictory parental communications concerning core gender identity, masculinity, femininity, and sexual role. . . . There is certainly no awareness of choice. (p. 179)*

I differ with McDougall only slightly—in the matter of emphasis more than content. That homosexualities—along with neosexualities—often seem to manifest themselves "addictively" is an observation that seems to me to bear a bit more investigation. Certainly McDougall tackles the question of sexual "addiction" in ways that illuminate much of what I know (from my own experience and from the experience of a huge number of sometimes self-described "addicted" gay men) to be true. In this addictive arena, McDougall says,

> . . . *sexual relations can come to represent a dramatic and compulsive way of preventing one's narcissistic self-image from disintegrating. The sexual act itself is used not only to dispel affective overcharge and to repair a damaged narcissistic image of one's gender identity, but also to deflect the forces of infantile rage from being turned back upon the self or against the internalized parental representations. Thus a drug-like utilization of sexuality becomes necessary to suspend feelings of violence as well as to anesthetize, if only temporarily, a castrated image of the self, a threatened loss of ego boundaries, or feelings of inner deadness. (p. 190)*

This description of the force of "addictive" sex has an undeniable ring of truth. What I would add, however, is that most gay men's experiences of compulsive sexual urges do wane and wax: sometimes we're compulsive, sometimes we're not. In other words, while extreme poles undeniably exist—ranging from a frightened celibacy to a frantic repetition of sexual acting-out—many (I would venture to say most) gay men move quite fluidly between these poles—always, as McDougall says, with the goal of self-preservation, but not always reacting to that goal with a fierce do-or-die compulsiveness. In my experience, and in the experience of the men you'll meet in this chapter, neosexualities are certainly compelling—reaching down to the deepest heart of us in their attempts to deal with fear and anxiety—but they are not necessarily compulsive; we *can* (and do) learn to exercise choice over them.

There are an infinite number of ways of coming to peace with the (inevitable) contortions of our infant experiences and the primal scenes and assumptions to which they give rise: neo-sexualities constitute various categories of them. What makes me question some of McDougall's implications about the compulsivity of neosexualities (e.g., fetishism and sadomasochism) are my own experience and my knowledge of the experience of other neosexualists, all of whom have come to greater peace—not, certainly, without a good deal of inner work—with their neosexual choices than McDougall seems to imply is possible. Certainly when a "neosexualist" first experiences the revelation that he's sexually turned on in ways disapproved of, even despised by, his family and culture, he is not going to feel very free about the prospect of acting on whatever sexual scenario compels him. A part of the "inner work" for many gay men requires a long and difficult passage to self-acceptance that may begin with a good deal of compulsive "acting-out." It's not surprising that when a gay man turned on by or interested in sadomasochistic sex first makes the tentative attempt to find a willing partner, he will likely feel a good deal of anxiety, fear of being "found out," fear that fuels secrecy and possibly compulsive behavior. But when he encounters the idea, which saturates such S&M magazines as *Drummer,* that S&M sex is fun, normal, and there are thousands of people into what he's into, that fear often considerably abates. Heterosexuals may be constitutionally incapable of appreciating what a boon they enjoy in the implicit and explicit cultural endorsement of heterosexuality: everything from chewing gum ads to church socials to sitcoms act out for them every rite of passage, proclaiming them as the soul of normality: heterosexuals are, in fact, in a *constant* state of reassuring each other that they're normal. (Paglia, Bersani, Browning, and Simpson have already helped us to examine the homophobia and repressed desires that may underlie that desperation.) This is, after all, one of the functions of culture: to normalize its own assumptions and standards to reinforce its own continuance. To perceive oneself as *bucking* the general culture (and the microcosm of your own terrifying family) is, at first, very scary stuff. It's no wonder if we have to battle through so much self-mistrust, even self-hate—which in turn fuel obsessions and compulsions about sex scenes and objects that we have been taught so generally to despise. In other words, it seems to me predictable that any neosexualist is going, initially, to have a hard time coming to any sort of peace with his neosexuality, not only for his own internal psychic reasons, but because of the profound disapproval he encounters in the world outside. Behavior that may quite plausibly be termed "addictive" is often a part—might be seen as a normal part—of this difficult passage to the neosexualist's eventual self-acceptance.

In an earlier book, *Theatres of the Mind,* McDougall says of people who are forced to create their own neosexualities that "we must necessarily assume that these unusual inventions, which usually come to light in adolescence, represent the best available explanation or sexual theory that the child was able to find in order to deal with overwhelming conflicts and contradictions." This prods me to think: What more could be expected? Any human being is doing "the best" he or she can do in his or her unconscious sexual choices. We're all dealt a lopsided hand of cards—some of us get spades, some of us get hearts; we have no choice but to play the hand we've been dealt.

In my experience (and in the experience of the gay men in this book), any "free" consciousness about sex is only ever fleetingly or imperfectly achieved. The best we can hope for—and it's a lot—is more of a sense of playfulness about the ogres and angels we discover in our formerly unconscious scenarios, more of a sense of being able to manipulate them in the playful way that Christopher Bollas describes. In other words, the best most of us can hope for is to discover a kind of "Pilgrim's Progress" sense of some of the largest most compelling aspects of our sexual universe, and play these allegorical characters and archetypes on a kind of chessboard, taking pleasure in them when we can, reminding ourselves that they *are* after all manipulable. (This seems to me to be the greatest gift of consciousness; it's my inducement to continue analysis for the rest of my life.) It's this sense of playfulness that can deliver us out of compulsive behavior: the more conscious we are of our internal universes, the more choices we feel we can exercise over them.

In the acting-out of my own sexual fantasies, I have ultimately discovered and experienced a greater, not a lesser, feeling of choice, and certainly a greater understanding—sometimes from the disappointment, even the heartbreak, of discovering that fantasy can't be made reality—of my "own private Idaho"—my own private sexual universe. My repertoire of choices hasn't constricted as a result of attempting to explore fantasy in the flesh; it has widened.

The triumph of "Eros" over "Thanatos" is never made easily or once-and-for-all: any route to this triumph is as individual and halting and fallible as the human being who pursues it. In *Theatres of the Mind,* Joyce McDougall offers her essential agreement with this idea: "As long as the dimension of reparation is maintained, deviant sexuality is able to avoid a psychotic solution to the conflicts, and Eros triumphs over death" (p. 283). A "dimension of reparation" is discovered and maintained when we start to feel choice about the exercise of our sexual fantasies; it seems to me that we can attain this dimension in an infinity of ways, and that we maintain it (as McDougall also says), with continual small successes and failures, advances and relapses, for the whole length of our lives. Every sexuality is at least metaphorically a "neosexuality": we each of us unconsciously create our own versions of the primal scene, and we're stuck with the demons, gods, ogres, and saints these scenes inevitably create in our sexual universes.

What better to do than follow Christopher Bollas's invitation to play with them?

THE USES OF COMPULSION

If there's one overarching, illuminating point I'd like us to coax from the foregoing, it's simply this: that we view sexual symptoms and fixations as the psyche's energetic and ingenious attempts to cure itself—to give itself what it craves. When we begin to explore the ingenuity with which the unconscious mind provides itself (and the rest of the conscious self) with exactly what it needs, we begin to respect the curative, reparative functions of fantasy. I stress (once again) that the more we're able to become conscious of this reparative impulse and function of our sexual fantasies and selves, the more choice and enjoyment and awe we can bring to the solutions our psyches continually, volcanically offer. We start to think less in terms of pathology and more in terms of literal self-help: we catch ourselves in the act of helping ourselves to discharge tensions sexually in ways that fit us to a T. In some now forgotten Agatha Christie novel, I came across this wonderful line, which I typed onto a piece of paper I then taped onto the top of my computer screen, to remind me of our human secret, ongoing psychic ingenuity: "One's unconscious is tremendously efficient." Thank you, Dame Agatha: that, in a sentence, is what I've been trying to say. I would add: "It has a genius for getting what it wants."

The emphasis on symptom-as-self-cure I take from psychoanalytic theory is dampened by much of what psychoanalysts tell us because of an obvious problem. Analysts' insights about human behavior are generally based on people who have come to them because they're troubled by their behavior—people who perceive themselves to be ill. Both Bollas and McDougall cite patients who have identified their behavior as a problem; it seems to me patently illogical to deduce from them any necessary truths about, say, all gay men who have anonymous and/or sado-masochistic and/or other forms of kinky sex. In fact, plenty of gay men have come to a quite fertile peace with themselves about their sexual behavior, however far from the mainstream it may seem to others to fall.

One of them is Ben. Ben died a few years back of a heart attack at the age of seventy-eight, after about five years of generally poor health. He was, to put it bluntly, a grumbling old cuss—and a hard man to like. People who knew him from AA meetings—he'd been sober for forty years by the time he died—recall cringing every time he opened his mouth. He had no patience with anyone who tried to psychoanalyze—when anyone talked about anything other than alcohol, he went into a tirade: "Nobody damned cares about your sick grandmother or whether you got a raise or not. This is an AA meeting, not group therapy. Talk about being sober or get the hell out of here and find a shrink." Not that Ben went to that many AA meetings: being around too many people for too extended a time seemed to chafe against him. Ben was a quintessential loner. "I know what I want," he once told me, "and I damned well know how to get it. And one thing I've learned is not to depend on anybody else to get it for me."

Actually, Ben did have a housemate—someone I later learned had been his lover decades before, for a very brief period: Andy, a man who is now in his late sixties and who nursed Ben through his last days. Andy is black, which gives an essential key to Ben's sexual tastes: as he once told me, "I love black dick. Always have, always will." Andy was quick to assure me that although Ben was born in Mississippi "and looked like a damned white-trash dirt farmer," his fixation on "black dick" was completely sexual and did not mean he was a bigot. "Believe me," Andy said, "I'd've been out of there like a shot if I thought he was. But you know, some men like Asians, some like swarthy Italian types, others like black boys—it's just how sex is, I guess." Ben also, by the evidence of his actions more than by his words, loved Andy—although their relationship was not sexual past what Andy later confided in me was the first six months of their relationship, Ben eventually signed over to Andy his house on Fire Island, left him all his money, and otherwise took care of Andy financially and, in his own way, emotionally for the thirty or so years they were together. Andy freely admits he's "an auntie. I taught public-school music for about twenty years until I retired in my fifties, and after made some money giving private piano and organ lessons. But basically I love to keep things in order. Ben was such a slob, he needed a keeper, and I guess that's what I became. You know, nobody much liked Ben because he always said exactly what he felt, and nobody likes quite that much honesty from anyone. But Ben was a rock. We loved each other more than you might think. I miss him terribly."

I base Ben's story on a few brief conversations I had with him, as well as Andy's reminiscences. But I also base it on what I sensed from Ben—a self-acceptance about as complete as any I've seen in a human being. One aspect of Ben's life overshadowed every other: he loved sex. He'd spend weeks of every winter in various Caribbean islands, from Puerto Rico to Haiti, "buying" black boy after black boy, taking Polaroid pictures of their dicks, and passing the snapshots around at the least provocation ("Whoa, mama, look at that one—you ever had a dick that big up your ass?"). "Dinner parties," Andy says, "were rarely the civilized affairs I wanted them to be. I'd fuss over the flow-ers and the candles and the soufflé, and Ben would bring out his personal pornography collection. And, my heavens, the things he'd take pictures of. . . . His favorite pictures were of group scenes—before Haiti exploded into all that political mess, he'd stay at a gay hotel there and literally rent a half dozen black boys from Port-au-Prince at a time, tell them all to strip, and instruct them to assume various untoward positions while he took pic-tures. He'd get himself into the scene, too, of course, and he'd have one or another of them take pictures of him—getting fucked, sucking one or another huge dick. I can't tell you the delight in Ben's eyes as he passed these pictures around at the din-ner table. He especially liked showing them to our more uptight guests, including one elderly woman who had been the princi-pal at the junior high I used to teach at. She took it remarkably calmly, I thought—didn't say a word, smiled primly, and talked about her own trips to the Caribbean. Ben was pissed as hell—he loved to shock people, make 'em turn red."

In the summers, Ben could be found every day between four and five-thirty in the afternoon and then again for an hour or so after midnight in Fire Island's meat rack—the woods be-tween the Pines and Cherry Grove, which have served as a sex-ual playground for gay men for the past fifty or more years. "Used to be," Ben said, "in the fifties, we'd have sex right in front of the houses late at night—you never knew what part of who you'd bump into; there weren't any lights. That's what I like—pitch-darkness and group scenes. Can't get enough." Ben was a fixture in the meat rack long into his seventies. Once he told me, "I know what the younger boys think of me. I even heard one of them say to his friend the other night, 'I sure hope I don't end up like him'—meaning me. I told that asshole: 'You should be so lucky.' "

Ben liked moving in on group scenes already in progress,

especially after midnight when they couldn't see how old he was—"you'd be amazed what hot boys will let you do to them in the dark. . . . I've had some great sex lately." In the winters, when he wasn't buying up rent boys in the Caribbean, he'd make daily sojourns to the baths, where he'd lurk in the shadows of his unlit room lying on his stomach, head toward the open door, waiting for passing penises like a fly in a web. "I give the best head in the Northeast," he'd proudly say. "Had a lot of practice. You don't like how I look? Close your eyes and stick out your dick. I'll make you see stars."

In one of his rare reflective moments, Ben once said that he knew other people would probably call him sexually compulsive—"that's the phrase you hear at gay AA meetings all the time," he said disgustedly—"and I know that ever since I stopped drinking, I've held on to sex as a way to keep sane. But, hell: it works. I'm not crazy. I know there's AIDS out there: I won't let one of my black boys fuck me without a condom. My smoking and heart condition will kill me after a while, but what the hell—I'm doing what I want to do. I just hope I go in the midst of getting fucked by some hot boy-stud. People don't like it? They can get fucked. Which is probably what they want to do anyway. I don't know why all so many gay boys have all this sex and then whine on and on about it later. Why don't they just enjoy themselves? If it gets out of hand, and okay, I know it can for some men, then stop having so much sex, take a cold shower, or even—though I never would—go to a shrink. But don't be a fuckin' hypocrite. I'll tell you, the reason I keep hauling out my pictures of hot black boys is to remind everyone in the room not only that I have a lot of sex, but that, usually, *they* are having a lot of sex, too—or want to. I just wish we'd all 'fess up to it. I see all these guys at AA meetings going on about what good little boys they are, and then I see the same guys on their knees, sniffing poppers, sucking one dick after another. Why don't they just say what they're doing? It doesn't have to be such an all-out weeping crisis. Gay men like to have sex. Big deal. Have it or don't have it, but don't keep whining on about it. Me? Call me a dirty old man—I don't mind. I'm having a fine time."

Ben was an unapologetic dirty old man even into his last years, as his health began to fade. Andy said that Ben had an arrangement with Larry, a young black college student who visited Ben even when he was bedridden and did what Andy called "an outrageous striptease in front of him while Ben beat off. He still came like he was an eighteen-year-old: his come hit the wall in back of him! He was always so happy when that boy came over. In fact, Larry had been to see him the morning of the day he finally passed away. He went the way he wanted to—with the memory of a beautiful naked man in front of him."

One other conversation with Ben sticks with me. I talked to him around my thirty-fifth birthday and (only half-jokingly) asked him to commiserate with me about getting too old to compete with younger men. But he'd have none of it. "Get over it," he said. "You had your day—now let the young guys have their day. Soon enough they'll be coming to you for some daddy fantasy, don't worry. You can still enjoy a beautiful boy—you don't have to be one." Ben was uncharacteristically loquacious on the topic; something here had hit a nerve: "Everyone has their day in the sun. I love to see new crops of arrogant boys hit the streets. I don't feel jealous of them. I know what it was like to be twenty-one and think you're the center of the universe. Let 'em enjoy themselves. It's their turn to be arrogant and hot. I don't know what all this stuff about attitude is—I think it's great that hot young boys walk around like they're untouchable gods. They *are* gods—why not let them enjoy it? They'll get old soon enough. Anyway, they're not gonna stop me from having fun. There's plenty of sex for everyone, doesn't matter how old you are. Sure, you may have to pay for it, but so what?"

My intuition about Ben was just as strong as anything he or Andy told me about the peace with himself he had come to: this was not a tortured, compulsive man. He was able to see himself as he was—and able to enjoy his absurdity, his outrageousness. As sexually obsessed as others may have seen him, he seemed to me to have incorporated his sexual adventures rather than be overcome by them. I don't know what he was like when he was arrogant and twenty-one: I certainly wouldn't be surprised if Ben knew his share of torture in his youth. His self-acceptance undoubtedly evolved through some stormy times: I knew from descriptions of his drinking days that he was once hell-bent on some pretty dangerous self-destruction (he wrecked at least one car while drunk, broke almost every bone in his body, and narrowly escaped with his life). But somehow, eventually, he'd managed to align himself with the propulsive self-destructive force in him—managed to channel it into what turned out to be a very exciting and satisfying life. That sex was the center of it isn't a reason to condemn that life: it simply gave him focus. As Quentin Crisp might say, "Sex was his style."

It doesn't, of course, always work so seamlessly for the rest of us. A central question I have had to face in my own life has to do with the notion of acting out: projecting terrifying feelings into somatic or bodily action. I have problems with the phrase *acting out* because it so dismissive—without really telling us enough about what is going on when we act out a feeling. How much was Ben acting out? How much less hold might sex have had over him had he been able to talk it out instead of fuck or suck it out? It is, for Ben, an unanswerable question; more, having known Ben, it seems to me an irrelevant question. Whatever acting-out function sex may have had for Ben, the acting out worked more than not for him. It occurs to me, reflecting on my own sexual experience, some of which I have at various times labeled compulsive, that there is a kind of blood-pressure rhythm and flow, a line we might imagine charting between Acting Out at, say, the bottom of a vertical range, and Consciously Enjoying Sex at the top of that range. The line is perpetually somewhere in the middle, sometimes swooping down at moments of greater anxiety, sometimes floating up at moments of greater peace. We all, by acting in any way whatsoever, in some sense act out unconscious urges and feelings: remember Agatha Christie's observation about the efficiency of the unconscious; *it's going to get what it wants.* The consciousness I've been calling for throughout this book is always, it seems to me necessarily, a relative consciousness. We're never going to know everything about why we crave what we crave. That blood-pressure line is always going to float somewhere below pure consciousness and somewhere above pure acting out.

Dennis, a twenty-eight-year-old self-described "Chelsea clone," vividly demonstrates what it means to get stuck at the lower end of this spectrum—the acting-out pole. "I call myself a Chelsea clone with some irony," says Dennis, a strikingly handsome blond man who works as a booking agent for a modeling agency in New York. "I mean, every Chelsea boy says he's not a Chelsea boy—we all have a lot of attitude about everyone else. But really, we're all competitive whores. What I'm really saying is that I know I'm smack in the middle of the race: I'm incredibly competitive with other guys out there. God, in the summer especially, they can drive me mad. There seem to be armies of shirtless, bronzed, perfectly muscled gods zooming on Rollerblades throughout the West Village and Chelsea, careful to make eye contact with no one, proclaiming their untouchable beauty to everyone. Sex, to me, is one big arena where you try to get the hottest one of these gods you can. It's total conquest. I know I'm good-looking, although I'm lousy on Rollerblades. But I can compete—and God knows, I do. I hit all the clubs, I'm out in the Pines every weekend. I've got plenty of notches on my belt, plenty of conquests in back of me. But it's getting—no, it's gotten—out of control."

Dennis admits to being as sexually obsessed as his elder, Ben, was, but he feels a lot less peaceful about it. "I have these recurring dreams, they're horrible. I start aging all of a sudden. I get some disease where my skin starts wrinkling, my teeth start loosening and falling out, I'm suddenly unable to move my body. They're dreams of what must be my worst fear, falling apart. I can't believe how clear they are. But the truth is, I *am* falling apart—maybe not yet physically, but emotionally. Until recently, my whole life revolved around what new hot guy I was going to get into bed—I've been completely obsessed with sex, or maybe more with power—everything's about conquest. It doesn't help that I work at this modeling agency: all they peddle, all they're interested in, is flesh. It's like the world only exists on the surface."

Dennis came to an abrupt halt recently when, as he says, "I found myself lying on the floor of a sex club at four in the morning, whacked out of my mind on Ecstasy and Special K, with various leather guys peeing on me and kicking me around with their boots. . . . It was the morning after Gay Day—the Stonewall parade—and I'd been out at bars and clubs all day and night, looking for the next thrill for hours and hours, checking myself out in every available mirror, comparing myself to every other guy I saw, unbuttoning my shirt until, by the time I was in that sex club, I was half-naked. It was like there wasn't anything I wouldn't do to get higher, get to a bigger thrill, get to some imagined unattainable prize of sex, of some impossibly hot man, some impossible solution to whatever this screaming hunger in me was all about."

Dennis shakes his handsome head in bewilderment. "I guess the drugs were finally wearing off, because I started to crash really badly, and I started to hate where I was and what was happening to me. The smell of urine and sweat was making me nauseous. I got up to go to some sink to wash myself off, determined to get the hell out of there and speed home. I'd never sunk so low, that's what it felt like. But as I got up, somebody grabbed my arm, and I turned around angrily to see who was daring to touch me. God, it was a guy in a wheelchair: he had no legs below his midthighs, the stumps of which you could see because he'd taken his pants and underwear off. The shock of him looking at me so hungrily, and the shock of those cutoff stumps of legs—for a moment I couldn't move. 'Please just stand there while I beat off?' he pleaded with me. And, because I couldn't move, I did stand there while he jacked himself off. I remember staring at his small, hard, uncut dick—between his body and his little cock he couldn't have had too much sexual attention from anybody before this. But something in his wide eyes—I can't explain what it did to me. It was like I was looking at myself, somehow. Physically he looked like how, in some way, I felt about myself: crippled, inadequate, starving for attention. Involuntarily my hand went out to touch his face—I felt this sudden feeling of tenderness toward him—but the second I made contact with him, he shot his load. He sighed deeply, like he was ashamed, and then looked down, away from me. He quickly wheeled himself away. But I still couldn't move. Various other guys were standing around, looking at me, obviously curious about why I'd shown this guy any attention. They didn't know I felt I'd come into contact with some part of myself."

If the story were simpler, Dennis said, "I would have seen the light and—I don't know—reformed or something. But things got worse after that. It was as if I had to prove to myself I wasn't that crippled guy in a wheelchair—the memory of his face, his eyes, his little dick, and the stumps of his legs somehow took center stage in my head. Maybe to erase that image, I don't know, I threw myself, for weeks afterward, into as much 'prestigious' sex as I could get. I'd go after the gods and tried to make each conquest mean I was—well, more than acceptable: safe. It was like the only way I could feel anything good about myself was to have sex with beautiful men—if I could attract a beautiful man, I couldn't be all bad. But finally, it's like I squeezed myself dry. Almost literally. The last guy I took home—I met him on the street, late at night—I couldn't function sexually. My dick just wouldn't respond. It's like it wasn't even my dick anymore. Something had just sort of closed down inside me, like a bank vault slamming shut. I think that's when the real despair hit—if I couldn't prove myself sexually, what worth did I have?"

Dennis began going to Sexual Compulsives Anonymous meetings, a listing for which he had seen in a gay paper. "I didn't know what to expect. I think, if anything, I was hoping I'd meet someone who was as driven as I was—maybe then I could respond sexually again! But it wasn't like that at all. I have some real problems with the whole twelve-step model, which SCA advocates—I'm uncomfortable with all that God talk, all that spiritual stuff. My radar is really on the alert for sexophobia—like some guys feel they're sober when they don't have any sex at all. Even masturbation for some guys is a sign that they've 'slipped.' I was really judgmental about it: what were they, crazy? But then I'd listen more closely to the stories. Like the guy who actually damaged his penis so severely, because he masturbated so violently and often, that he had to go for medical treatment. Or another guy who got so in debt from sex-phone lines and prostitutes that he tried to kill himself—he just saw no way of stopping. There were other stories that made me feel like Rebecca of Sunnybrook Farm—I didn't have an edge on sexual compulsion. So many gay men seemed to be wrestling with it. It was a good place for me, after all, because I began to see and have some compassion for the desperation that kicked so many of our butts. We all were hungry for something, and the only way we knew how to respond to that hunger was to grab for whatever we could, as quickly as we could, whenever we could. My own hunger became clearer to me. I saw that when my dick stopped working, something inside of me was trying to get my attention. 'Stop,' it seemed to say. 'This is not getting what you need!' It wasn't my dick that refused to cooperate, it was something deeper in me: I'd even call it my soul."

Dennis has also found SCA rewarding because it's given him a forum to talk about his confusion and has bolstered a new insight. "I see that I was trying to get from physical looks, physical bodies, skin, asses, dicks, faces, hair, something all that just isn't equipped to give me. It's like I was a baby screaming that I couldn't get milk in a hardware store—to paraphrase a line you hear a lot in SCA meetings. I had to look elsewhere for what I really needed. And what this has done—well, I've turned into someone for whom celibacy, right now, is sexual sobriety. Those guys I used to sneer at secretly who felt wonderful because they'd gone six days without masturbating: incredibly, I've become one of them! It's just that any sex, right now, is going to be an explosion I'm just not strong enough to withstand. It's important for me to talk about sex, not have it. I know I'll be sexual again, sometime—who knows, maybe with someone I actually get to know first! But not until I think I can handle it without going crazy. I guess what all this amounts to is, I've called time-out. It's not easy—my first impulse is still, and probably always will be, to jump right back into the sexual circus and start fucking every god I can get my hands on. But I'd be lost if I did that now. So, with the help of friends I've met at SCA, I won't. One day at a time, as they put it. Oh, you might be interested to hear something else. That guy in the wheelchair has started coming to meetings. His name is Jack. He's a nice guy. And I can't tell you the look of shock and then relief on his face when he saw me. I think we might actually turn into friends."

Developing the consciousness we've explored in this book may sometimes lead you to take time-out in the way Dennis has described. His story also reminds us that we can depend on our emotional, bodily, and psychic reactions to tell us when something is wrong, or when it's right. Dennis's dick's "shutting down" is another instance of his unconscious trying to flag him down: *Pay attention to me!* The conscious mind's relation to the waning and waxing of a penis—which doesn't give a damn about what the conscious mind thinks about those wanings and waxings—will, in fact, be our next topic. Paying attention to your dick doesn't mean damning it for popping up when you don't want it to, or not popping up when you do. The whole issue of "potency" is a much more subtle business.

THE USES OF IMPOTENCE

First, problems with "impotence"—which I put in quotes because I think it's a silly and, worse, misleading term for not being able to get an erection on demand—may be even less talked about among gay men than they are among straight men. Actually, what we call impotence can offer some very potent information about us. "Hell," one friend of mine, Gary, says, "they've got whole books addressed to straight men about potency. A gay guy who can't get it up is even more of a pariah than a straight guy. I mean, sex is the one thing gay men are supposed to be good at, right? But what about when you're not good at it? Like me."

Gary, thirty-two, from a small town in Ohio that, he says, "Madison Avenue must have had in mind in the 1950s when they conceived the perfect market for Velveeta, lime Jell-O, and

Skippy peanut butter," went to college in the San Francisco area in the early eighties, right "when all the sex clubs were closing down and everyone was getting paranoid about AIDS. In a way, I was relieved that there might be less pressure to have the wild sex that put gay San Francisco on the map. I was just coming out, and it seemed that you couldn't get into the gay world without being some whiz at this or that nth-degree sexual practice. Looking through sex magazines told me I had to want to have marathon sucking and fucking sessions, or get fisted up the ass or drink piss or be tied up while someone put clamps on my nipples and dripped hot wax on my dick. When I first went to bars, I couldn't help wondering what all of these relatively mild-looking men were really fantasizing about—the truth was, I was scared shitless of them. More accurately, scared that there was no way I could perform the way I imagined every other out gay man had somehow magically learned to do. I didn't have sex with anyone for a year and a half after coming out—which I did mostly in my head. I tried various social situations—joined a square dance club, which had a lot of great people, many of whom have turned into friends, nearly all of whom are lesbians. No sex with that bunch. . . . I was curious about the few remaining anonymous venues for sex. For instance, sometimes I'd cruise Golden Gate Park, but with the secret determination not to look at anyone who looked at me. I wanted the idea of sex more than the actual act itself. I just didn't feel equal to it. I guess another part of it is that I'm no Adonis. I have a nice enough dick, I suppose, but my body is just sort of columnar—average, with a little belly. I'm losing my hair a bit, which I understand some guys think is hot—at least it means my testosterone is doing its thing—but all it does is make me self-conscious. I actually eventually had one 'sort of' relationship. I answered the least intimidating personal ad I could find in one of San Francisco's gay papers. It was from a guy who described himself as quiet, liked to read, curl up in

front of the fire, wasn't into the bar scene, was looking for someone affectionate. He sounded like a sort of sweet, friendly dog to
me, which is what he pretty much was. After a number of chaste
movie, dance, and theater dates, Jerry and I went to bed, and he
was as affectionate as he said he was, but the second his hand got
anywhere near my dick, I froze. As nonintimidating as Jerry was,
he was still sexual, which I could tell because his dick was jab-
bing me in the leg, as hard as mine would never be. It's like I
simply closed shop in my groin. I didn't feel anything, except,
eventually, frightened and even annoyed at Jerry for continuing
to try to arouse me when it was clear I just wasn't having any."

After another couple of "my dick not showing up when I
did" overnight dates, Gary gave up and broke up with Jerry.
"Jerry kept feeling it was that I wasn't attracted to him, which
was sort of true, but not in the way Jerry feared. I couldn't release feelings of attraction for anybody, not just Jerry. It's not that
I didn't have a kind of fantasy, I did and do, but it's so sort of
vague and amorphous; it doesn't seem to translate into anything
I can actually do with anyone. What turns me on, in the privacy
of my own head, is really more voyeurism than actual sex.
Watching a guy take his clothes off, slowly, savoring every new
naked inch of him each discarded piece of clothing reveals. That's
what I beat off to—just looking. I think of my junior and senior
high locker rooms, and the times at college when I'd go to the
swimming pool and linger in the changing room sneaking looks
at men stripping. It seemed incredible to me that all these guys
got naked in front of each other and weren't just staring at how
beautiful they all were. Not that I ever got an erection in a locker
room. Again, being in the presence of an actual human being
slams the door on the blood flow to my penis—it's just too
frightening to me."

Although he couldn't believe his chutzpah, about five years
ago Gary drummed up his courage and decided to "rent" a man,

fixating on a particularly beautiful photograph of a college-age kid who was advertising his wares in a sex magazine. "I thought, okay, if what I really want is just to look at a man take off his clothes, why don't I just pay one to do it, and, well, practice masturbating in front of him. It seemed almost therapeutic." Gary hired the guy (stopping himself mid-dial six times before letting the phone ring), who came over within the hour. Gary stammered out that he "sort of liked to watch guys undress and if 'Buck' didn't mind, could he just do, you know, a striptease or something? I mean, only if he wanted to." Gary laughs. "I was such a wimp. Buck had probably had several gerbils up his ass an hour before, and here I was politely asking him to take his clothes off—'only if he wanted.' Buck was beautiful—smooth, blond, clean-cut, with a pornographic-sized dick, and he actually got into the striptease—peeling off his T-shirt, slipping off his pants, and easing down his Calvin Klein's like the pro he was. I didn't even take my pants off. I just unzipped and sort of groped around inside looking for Mr. Goodbar, who still wasn't having any. Here I was hiring someone and I still couldn't get an erection. Well, it probably didn't help that the man was so pornographically perfect. It just widened the gap between the idea of a sex object and the fallible, soft little things me and my dick were."

This experience precipitated a bad depression for Gary. "There didn't seem to be any solution. While I was fixated on not being able to perform sexually, I knew the problem went deeper. I didn't relish the idea of wallowing in a lot of psychological shit about my sexless parents, but they were sexless—good Methodists who rarely kissed each other, certainly displayed a minimum of physical affection to anyone—including me. Sex just didn't exist for me growing up. But I couldn't seem to connect with anybody on any level, not just sexually. I started, after the humiliating Buck experience, to hate myself. It was like I wasn't even human. Something really essential had been left out of me—some ability to feel." Gary's depression got so bad that eventually he sought help for it. "I found an ad for a gay psychotherapist in yet another gay paper and met with him, liked him, and through his counsel, got on Prozac and into all that 'psychological shit' I'd been avoiding for so long. The Prozac helped—it took the edge off the despair, made it manageable—but if anything it seemed to tamp down my sex urge even more. The difference was, I just didn't care very much that my dick rarely rose; I got to the point where I wasn't even masturbating. But I was talking, for the first time in my life, about these feelings of being cutoff, this terrible void in the center of me. My therapist became a central part of my life, I suppose just because he seemed to listen, and not judge."

After about a year of being on medication and going to his therapist, Gary decided, now that the worst of his depression seemed to have lifted, to give the gay urban sexual arena another try. "By this time, jack-off clubs were the new hot thing, and I began to fantasize out loud to my therapist about what a sexy idea that was—all these guys, like the kids in my school locker rooms, just walking around playing with their dicks. It just didn't seem as intimidating as the rest of gay male sex. Eventually my therapist said, 'Why don't you go sometime?' And so I did. One Saturday night, I took a shower, put on my favorite pair of Calvin Klein briefs—I've got a thing for them, ever since I saw how Buck looked in them—and wore the de rigueur T-shirt, jeans, and boots costume that constituted gay male mufti. I told myself that I didn't have to take my clothes off, that I could just sit there with a can of soda and watch if I wanted to. I kept chanting reassurances to myself as I took the bus to the sex club: it's gonna be all right, you don't have to do anything. . . . I got there fairly early and was horrified to find that there was a mandatory clothes check. I managed to stammer to the guy at the door, 'Could I keep on my underwear?' He nodded yes, and suddenly I found myself in a dark room with little side hallways and cubbyholes, too dark at first for my eyes to make anything out. I stripped out of my jeans and T-shirt and boots and handed them to a guy behind a desk marked Clothes Check and wandered into the room. What I saw was amazing. It wasn't crowded yet, but already, groups of men were sort of huddling into each other in the corners, exactly like dogs sniffing each other out. I love watching dogs smell each other's asses—they do it as such a matter of course. It's just how they greet each other. Well, something similar was going on here. Tentatively I walked over to one of the larger groups, standing at the periphery. As my eyes adjusted, I saw about ten men, a couple of them old and potbellied, a couple young college-type kids, the rest sort of normal-looking guys in their thirties—no pornographic princes, which put me at some sort of relative ease. But the feeling I got looking at these guys stroking their dicks, sometimes stroking each other's chests or asses, moving in close so that their dicks were all pointing inward and it sort of didn't matter whose dick was whose: ah! That was it. It was like all these men's bodies sort of melded into a larger unit. It didn't matter who touched whom, there was nothing but a kind of animal clustering, like babies exploring each other in complete innocent, curious wonder. Then one of the midthirties guys reached out and caressed my ass, gently slipping his hand under my briefs. Another older man reached over and played with my left nipple. I was ushered into the center of the group. It was the most wondrous feeling: the smell of these men, a heady mix of deodorant and cologne and a faint smell of sweat, the warm male animal caressing, so gentle, so undemanding, and yet so eager and hungry and curious—it was like my whole body was learning to be erotic. As much as this was a jack-off club, the focus was, for me, for once, not on the dick. It was on male flesh meeting male flesh. I got so into feeling the muscular shoulder of a college kid next to me, and getting off on someone's gentle, warm, strong hand on my back, another man brushing my thigh with his thigh, that I didn't notice, at first, my own growing erection. Some door had opened. It was as if my dick, for the moment, had become too curious about this new erotic feeling not to respond. There was no reason not to. But I guess it came about because, finally, for once, I wasn't requiring anything of my dick. My whole body had eroticized, as did the whole bodies of the men brushing and nuzzling me now. Sex wasn't a matter of penile acrobatics: it was a pure matter of touch."

Translating this insight into "an actual relationship with one actual other person" is something Gary continues to work on. "I'm seeing that my fear of touching and being touched by another man—whose name I know, who is not a part of some anonymous group—isn't just that my dick won't pop up when I want it to. There's something about being seen by someone that scares me: it's like I can't help but feel I'll be judged as inadequate. This feeling of inadequacy isn't going to go away overnight. But somehow the feeling of sexual release and joy and connection I found at that jack-off club has given me a glimpse of a larger goal: to learn to feel that same easy, wide permission about the rest of who I am. It's this: I know connection is possible now, even if I still can't always achieve it. But I *am* a part of the human race. I can learn to touch and be touched, too. Which means there's now hope I once didn't dare to believe I could ever feel."

Dephallicizing sex is something a variety of gay men and queer theorists have thought about and explored. It is a liberating idea—that sexuality can be displaced from the phallus onto other parts of the body or bodily activities that don't directly involve the penis. Partly because so many gay men have been so fixated on The Cock, the invitation to sexualize—take equally intense pleasure in—other body parts and functions widens the canvas, expands libidinal possibility, promises a larger field of sexual exploration. Diffusing sex onto nongenital areas of the body can jostle and free the sexual imagination. Michael Foucault is especially invoked in this regard; e.g., a discussion with Foucault that appeared in the *Advocate* in 1984 (which Bersani cities in *Homos*) has him praising S&M practitioners for "inventing new possibilities of pleasure with strange parts of their bodies." As Bersani says, "he called S/M 'a creative enterprise, which has as one of its main features what I call the desexualization [which Bersani reads as degenitalization] of pleasure.' " Gary's experience shows us his route to this wider realization; he tells us from his experience that much more can become erotic than the penis— something, of course, most gay men know, from the urgings of their fantasies, on their own.

But the freedom to eroticize other parts of the body or the animate or inanimate world (as in fetishism) does not always, or perhaps ever, at first feel very free. When Apollo shoots up out of a gay man's chthonian darkness, his destination can seem very peculiar to those who don't share that gay man's particular section of chthonian muck. Once again, sexual fantasies and fixations are psychic attempts, unconscious attempts, at self-cure, as peculiar to our needs and drives and defenses as our handwriting. Gary's story gives us a principle that I think speaks to many of us—that sex can involve much more than getting a hard dick on demand, and that much more is potentially erotic than the penis—but the roots of Gary's fixations and fears and attempts at self-cure are unique to him. Respecting that our own psychic/sexual routes are just as urgently individual can make it a lot easier, not to say a lot more fun, to review, for example, the hold fetishes have on us. These neosexual choices (to echo McDougall's term) may force themselves on us unconsciously, but by taking a step back and looking at them, we can learn to feel more awe about their mission and enjoy more of the sheer damned pleasure they can give.

CODA: FETISHES

Sheer damned pleasure has a very specific meaning to Angelo, twenty-six, a self-proclaimed "proud Italian American," who, from his earliest memories, has always been riveted by men's sheer socks. "I mean the see-through nylon kind—my favorite are 'thick-and-thin' over-the-calf—the socks that working-class immigrant types wear when they dress up." This gives a clue about the roots of Angelo's fixation: "My dad is second-generation Italian, a real macho guy who first worked in construction, then ran his own hardware store. I remember—God, I must have been about four or five—him tickling my belly with his socked foot, sort of teasing me with it. The smell of shoe leather, the smell of his foot, the look and feel of that sheer material—I can't tell you what it did to me, and what the same thing does to me now. A macho guy wearing something almost feminine, a guy who curses and fights and struts around putting on this sort of pretty stuff . . ." He sighs and shakes his head. "The combination blows me away." Angelo says that, from about twelve on when he learned to masturbate, he'd dig into his parents' clothes hamper and find his dad's sheer socks, which he then wrapped around his cock while he jerked off. "Then I'd rinse them out and dry them in my closet—sheer socks dry real quick—and put them back in the hamper. I would've died if anyone had caught me."

Angelo says that while his main fixation is on sheer socks, "I've also sort of fetishized the whole man that goes with them. You know, sharp dressers. Guys when they go out on a date who dress up like peacocks. You wanna know what I'm talking about? See *The Pope of Greenwich Village*—Mickey Rourke makes me nuts in that one—or *The Wanderers*. Ken Wahl may not be Italian, but he sure looks like one." Angelo, who grew up in Brooklyn—"but not," he sighs wistfully, "Bay Ridge"—would, as a teenager, take subway trips to Bay Ridge with a Polaroid camera he'd gotten for his birthday, hang out in pizza shops, and pretend to take pictures of "street scenes, like I was some kind of artist or sociologist or something. I'd prepared all kinds of speeches about the 'surveys' I was researching in case anyone asked me what I was doing, but nobody did. Of course, what I was really taking pictures of were hot guys walking by, hoping to get a peek at their ankles. Man, one time this guy stopped right in front of the pizza place, leaned against the door, and slipped off a low-slung Italian loafer—I love those, too—and slowly massaged his sheer-socked foot, like he knew I was watching him. I nearly came in my pants." Angelo would haunt "cheap, lower-class" men's shops in search of "perfect pairs of thick-and-thins in every color I could find. Just wearing them would give me a hard-on all day. I also loved going to Italian weddings. Man, you had all these hot Italian macho peacocks strutting around—it was like heaven." He pauses a moment and frowns. "But it was also sort of like hell. I mean, the guys I was turned on by almost had to be straight. And there was no way I could share this with anyone. Jesus, my dad would've had me locked up."

Angelo went to college—the first of his family to do so—in considerable despair. "I knew this sock thing wasn't something I was going to grow out of. But I didn't know what to do about it. I could imagine coming out—well, not to my family, at least not yet—but I could imagine, you know, having a lover and being gay and all that. But I couldn't imagine even letting a lover know about what really turned me on. I felt so much shame about it. And then I met Danny." Danny was a junior; Angelo was still a freshman. "I saw him stride across campus and my heart stopped. He had this incredible macho confidence—he was so friggin' arrogant! Like he knew he was beautiful, like he knew he could wear clothes like a model. He had beautiful, thick, slicked-back black hair and blue eyes, and he moved like a dancer. I'd never seen anyone so beautiful, not even in Bay Ridge." Angelo hung out at the college's coffeehouse when he saw that Danny went there every day after his last afternoon class. "One day I had the nerve to walk up to him and say hi. I had some lame opening line like, 'I'm new here and you seem to really know the place. I was wondering if you could tell me how good the psychology department is.' I mean, it really was that lame. Danny just looked at me and laughed. He must have seen how lovestruck I was. He told me to sit down. Then his eyes bored into me and made me weak in the knees: 'Psychology what you're really asking me about?' I literally couldn't speak. Then he asked—the nerve of the asshole!—'You gay?' "

It turned out—"incredibly," Angelo says, "given what a macho, straight-looking stud he was"—that Danny was gay, which he abruptly told Angelo. "That was Danny, all over—blunt as hell. Totally comfortable with being gay—it was a fact like his eye color." Angelo found himself saying that, yes, he thought he might be gay. Danny and he then found themselves, not a half hour later, in Danny's bed. "I have never fallen so completely and totally in love with anyone in my life," Angelo said. "Danny just overwhelmed me. He was like a dream come true, a gay man who excited me as much as—no, even more than—the hottest Bay Ridge stud I'd ever seen. He was Puerto Rican, not Italian, but that was just fine with me. And God, the way he dressed!"

Danny was meticulous about his clothes. Angelo hoped that he was meticulous in the way Angelo hoped he'd be about his socks. "That was when my heart fell. Danny liked wearing simple, comfortable cotton socks. It was the only practical thing about him or his wardrobe. I mean, everything else was either fine silk and flowing gabardine, or when he was feeling slutty, spandex bike pants and skintight muscle Ts. Damn it—I had come so close to my ideal. It made me hate myself even more. Why were socks so damned important to me? Why couldn't I just sort of lighten up about it and get over it and thank God for what I'd found in Danny? But, I hate to say it, it was hard for me to get aroused with Danny because he wasn't wearing the kind of sheer socks that turned me on. It started to be a real problem. I mean, I wouldn't even get hard sometimes when we'd have sex. Finally, I remember it was a rainy November night, we were walking back from the dining hall, and he suddenly turned to me and asked me what the hell was wrong. My dick and he had a very close relationship: by staying limp, it was telling him more than I was." Angelo's face is tense as he relived what happened next. "It was pouring now, but I didn't care. We both were sopping wet, but I couldn't move out of the rain—I was going to take a risk I'd never taken before in my life, and it made my knees lock. I know it sounds silly now—like, why couldn't I have just told him? But I was eighteen, and I'd felt *so much* shame about this. I started to cry. Then I just blurted it out: 'I like socks!' There was silence for a moment. Danny looked confused. 'Well, so do I,' he said. 'In fact, mine are getting soaked at the moment.' I told him he didn't understand—that I liked a *certain kind* of socks. And then I told him everything, everything about my father, and beating off with his sheer nylon socks, and my trips to Bay Ridge, and my Polaroid collection of hot men taking their shoes off—the whole thing. I don't know what I expected from Danny. Probably to have him call me sick and just walk away from me. But he didn't do that. He just listened to me and then, when I was done, said, 'So, give me a pair!' And that was it for him. It wasn't any big thing. I was more stunned by this than anything else. How could he not think I was sick? I mean, this was real loony-bin stuff, wasn't it?"

The idea that it might be okay not only to talk about his

fetish but also to incorporate it into their sex life was a huge revelation for Angelo. "I'll always love Danny. Hell, we broke up about two years later. We ended up having horrendous fights—we both were kids, we didn't know shit about relationships—we fought about stupid stuff, but not about socks. But he taught me that I could love a part of myself I had always hate, felt such fear and shame about. He opened up the rest of my life—it doesn't seem too strong to say that. I'll always love him."

Fetishes are fascinating phenomena—condensed manifestations of that psychic attempt at self-cure we've been exploring throughout this book. Freud saw fetishes as displaced phalluses—because of some trauma that caused ungovernable terror of the primal scene (mommy and daddy copulating), the fetishist would, for a variety of fascinating, idiosyncratic reasons, eroticize some body part or other object and invest it with the power of genital sex, which he was too terrified to confront head-on. According to this idea, a sheer-socked foot is for Angelo a disguised, potent penis. This may have some validity. But it's not necessarily pathology. Even a quick look at the history of sex tells us this displacement is probably the most common aspect of our sexuality: in fact, the history of sex might be said to be a history of fetishes. Look at fashion over the last century: bustles fetishizing the buttocks, the sight of an ankle, which could make a man (or a lesbian) swoon, in the 1890s; androgynized women in the 1920s, their boyish figures, bobbed hair, and (above all) knees all fetishized; decades of variously emphasizing different hair lengths, hips, shoulders, breasts, asses, waists, thighs in women (Theda Bara to Garbo to Betty Grable to Marilyn Monroe to Cher to Sharon Stone); shoulders, waists, butts, crotches, height, hair length, etc., in men (Valentino to Gary Cooper to Brando to Brad Pitt): these all indicate body parts, emphasized through different styles of dress, that society tacitly agreed to fetishize. The current gay male fashion for goatees and baseball caps is one more fascinating example: the goatee sexualizing, fetishizing, the mouth as if with pubic hair (as if framing a vagina, an asshole), the art-fully curved brim of the cap jutting out like a proud erection—when it isn't worn backward in an attitude of submission (freeing the vagina/asshole/mouth to imbibe cock). These styles of dress and facial hair are only not (usually) called fetishes because they are shared by so many people at once; which, of course, is an ad-equate operative definition of "normal"—anything shared by the majority.

There is always objectification in sex. We invest people, body parts (breast, buttock, penis, among every other imaginable one), shoes, jockstraps, panties, socks, and an infinite number of other objects with erotic power for very interesting reasons, but the in-vestment *always* happens. Can you come to orgasm without some form or manner of objectification? It is always that final touch of a hand, a thigh, a foot, that final surge of the dick head you're staring at or fantasizing about, that final swish of satin or chiffon, that final whiff of leather, that final slice of the whip, that final infinitesimal but infinitely *specific* physical detail of fantasy that pulls the trigger. A sex object must be literally that: an ob-ject. It must be something powerful and containable; something that threatens with buried force (danger, taboo, shame are all part of what makes the erotic riveting; giving them up completely is the annihilation of sex), but which objectification makes finally safe and manipulable. It is, once again, Apollo battling Diony-sus, tight form restraining volcanic content, both winning in the roar and arc of orgasm.

Pat Califia, in the wake of describing the peculiar erotic thrill of using lubed latex gloves as sexual aids, muses eloquently on all this in her book *Public Sex:*

> *Why, oh why, is this sexy? I'm not going to answer*
> *that question by constructing a theory about infantile trauma*

caused by soggy Pampers and Mommy's cold hands. Psy-
choanalytic theories about the origins of sexual preferences
never give you hypotheses that can be operationally defined
and proved or refuted. Instead what you get are moral state-
ments about the inferiority of "the other" or recycled versions
of your own sexual prejudices. . . . The more we know about
what people do, the more we can understand how that be-
havior functions in their lives—what the rewards, stresses and
penalties are." (p. 192)

In emphasizing, and celebrating, the necessary objectification of sex, the ubiquity of fetishes, the peculiar balances of
chthonian darkness and Apollonian form that define our erotic
fantasies and lives, we've perhaps given the "rewards" of sex an
unfairly greater share of attention than the "stresses and penalties." Indeed, we cannot gloss over the fact that gay men are
sometimes tortured by the overwhelming power of sex and sexual fixations. There is, God knows, such a thing as mental pain—
severe enough, sometimes, to be called psychosis. The experience of addiction—e.g., to drugs, alcohol, and sex—is common
to a huge number of gay men. The triage of going to a twelve-
step meeting or seeking psychiatric help in the form of therapy
or medication is sometimes necessary—sometimes literally to
save your life. But I hope to have opened the psychic door on
this, too—to show that the forces we battle, whether or not they
result in what we might label addiction, are primal and complicated and deserving of our closest nonjudgmental attention. I've
written a great deal about recovery and talked to so many gay
men about their own experience of it. As I go on, I see recovery as far more than a means of figuring out how to get through
a day without a drink or a drug or a sex fix. It's an opening to
an entirely new, often frighteningly new, way of managing life,
requiring the kind of self-examination and even spiritual growth

that many nonaddicts are never booted into doing. To stay sober, you have to grow. The psychoanalytic part of this is that I see, much more clearly now than ever before, how deep the roots of the pain behind (at least the psychological causes of) alcoholism and drug addiction are: they go back, Freud tells us, to the earliest moments of life—the oral stage. Managing wounds suffered at this period of inchoate life as adults presents some particularly daunting challenges. We need to heed feelings more than words as we grow, because the wounds we need to heal came before we had language to understand or give perspective to them. Alcoholics and addicts battle a kind of psychosis—the psychosis of a terrified and raging infant—for all of their lives. But it's a battle, moment to moment, we can win, by cultivating our consciousness of and curiosity about the soldiers that are fighting it.

Sometimes the battle, this psychosis, hits us like a tidal wave: it may seem impossible to survive. It's as if the psyche's attempt to cure itself becomes blind to the life drive and now serves only death. I once knew a man with advanced AIDS who left ads on phone sex lines advertising himself as a "scum bucket." Giving his address to anyone who called, he simply left his door open, turned out the light, and proceeded to suck the cock and swallow the semen of anyone who walked in. This was his whole life. Nothing else existed for him. Apollo slowly drowned in chthonian darkness. The man was nothing but his gaunt eyes, gaping mouth, and sore, fragile knees. A recent perusal of New York's "Hardcore" sex line produced an ad, a serious ad, for a "snuff scene." The advertiser didn't care how you did it, you could get your kicks in any way you wanted to, as long as it ended in his death.

We are in psychotic territory not only with the stories of these men (and we could all tell each other many even sadder examples), but in the realms of our own sexual universes. The ability to dance around the volcano—not flee its flanks or throw yourself into it—is almost always hard won; the balance it requires is one each of us achieves in an individual way. What could kill one man might be the solution for another. You've seen the potential benefit of groups like Sexual Compulsives Anonymous; you've seen the help that therapy and medication can offer. When the urge to throw yourself into the bubbling crater gets too overwhelming to resist, you may feel you need to take options that abruptly muzzle and lock up the raging sexual beast that wants to jump. (Dennis experienced this: SCA was a kind of necessary triage for him.) But you've also met Ben, and Angelo, who, along with so many other men in this book, have found ways to dance even when the ground gets hot. There can be unbelievable life, pleasure, and revelation in that dance, and the strangest couplings: Apollo may actually waltz with Dionysus. The danger is inescapable, indeed, a certain amount of it fuels our richest sexual awakenings. Risk must be balanced with consciousness and self-care, but when it is—when Jekyll is allowed to kiss Hyde full on the lips—we experience sex as (what Joseph Campbell calls) "the burning point of life." And it doesn't get much better than that.

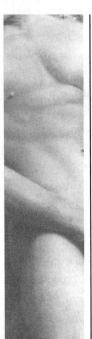

FIVE

"THIS IS IT, KID: SING"

The world exists because we love it.
—Jonathan Lear

THE ABOVE SINGLE SENTENCE FROM
Love and Its Place in Nature does no justice to Jonathan Lear's intensive exploration of Freud, psychoanalysis, and the power of love that the book so richly provides. But the quote does offer a summation of the arc these pages have so far followed. We've seen in virtually every man we've met a similar aha! moment: the discovery that, by becoming more conscious of the primal forces of sex and life and death that impel and propel each of us, by learning to heed the peculiar ways they manifest in our psyches, we can begin, in Christopher Bollas's words, to create a "generative asylum" that "allows the subject to play with the samples of reality that pass by him during his lifetime." As we discover, name, and investigate the feelings, archetypes, and fantasies that fill our sexual universes, we develop an ability to *play* in them,

find ways to ride the waves without falling off our Apollonian surfboards, find ways to "love" even the fiercest, most threatening components of our inner psychic landscapes. The more conscious we become, the more our worlds take shape: we create our worlds by learning to see, then love them.

The passage from this kind of self-love to loving another human being might be thought of as the next step—anyway, a challenge that is daunting in some different ways from the challenge of achieving the more purely *self*-acceptance that has been our focus so far. The accomplishment of a full, ringing narcissism is, as I've suggested, an important and generative one for gay men: which may just be another way of saying "you've got to love yourself before you can love anyone else." But how do we arc from this generative self-love to connecting with another man?

THE CHALLENGE OF
MEN MARRYING MEN

I hear a Niagara roar of deep sighs: *this* may be the roughest road ahead of us. Indeed, it can be tempting to follow the example of the elegantly self-realized and serenely autonomous Quentin Crisp, who, when I asked him in our book *The Wit and Wisdom of Quentin Crisp* if it was possible to be fulfilled in "marriage," replied:

"If your view is that your style—your image—is to be self-sacrificing, and if you feel you have an infinite capacity for sacrificing yourself, then you may think: Will I go to India to feed the starving, or to Crimea to bind up the wounds of the injured— or will I just get married?"

Self-sacrifice is undoubtedly one of the cornerstones of sustaining any marriage; it's the reason we find marriage a bitch. (Pop psychologists try to soften the blow by advocating compromise, a word the evasive, euphemistic connotations of which I'm not too fond, which we'll talk about later on.) But we may be able to link our foregoing explorations of individual self-acceptance a bit less abruptly to the idea of marriage—devoted, emotional, sexual, and sometimes monogamous relationships between two gay men—with the help of Frank Browning, who writes in *The Culture of Desire:*

> *On balance I wonder whether by making sex ordinary, even recreational, we have learned to re-form it into a tool for building diverse forms of comradeship. By stealing sex away from the restrictive laws of marriage, by acknowledging its myriad meanings, gay men may have shown how lust contributes to the bonds of friendship. By devaluing the taboo of sex among friends, they may have begun to shine more light on the complex and various ways intimacy can be arranged in emerging gay families. This is not to deny that lust without constraint can be abusive, callous, selfish, and ignoble; the point is only that through the persistent exploration of love and lust and nurturing, gay people have helped to open up the territory of family meanings. Individual gays and lesbians may not be able to create new "traditions" of mateship and friendship in family life. But their determination to find a new sort of family may well provide vital models for the remaking of all families, straight or gay. (pp. 156, 157)*

With Browning's help, I've slipped the word *families* into this discussion because it seems to me that any notion of marriage between gay men grows out of our peculiar experience of creating non-blood-tie families and connections. Many of us enter one-on-one relationships after a more or less wide experience of recreational sex, sex with friends or acquaintances or anonymous men, as well as nonsexual friendships with a huge variety of people—male, female, young, old, from school or work or social activities. We're not generally set up by our biological families to meet "the right man": we come to our romantic relationships with a feeling of winging it, of starting from scratch, of having few models on which to base whatever marriage we may want to enter into. No showers or stag parties for most of us—no wedding gifts and pats on the back from long-unseen uncles and aunts. Instead, the adrenaline impulse to connect we often feel might be summed up by what Esther Blodgett (aka Judy Garland) said her daddy told her in the "Born in a Trunk" sequence of *A Star Is Born* as he shoved her out to do her first solo: "This is it, kid: sing." (And what does she sing? "I'll get by—as long as I have you. . . ." With so little prep work and societal backup, it's perhaps no wonder that *we* often put so much pressure on whatever "you" we've decided is our only way to "get by.")

But many of us eventually construct social networks of friends and lovers, searching in them for what guidance and corroboration we can scrape together: the unions that grow out of these pioneer families and groups of friends can have a special and touching quality, and a good deal of groundbreaking form.

I wasn't really aware of it until each member of the group started getting sick and dying of AIDS, but I was privileged to see and learn to value the ties of an extraordinary group marriage of six gay men, friends whom I knew through an ex-lover with whom I lived for twelve years. The fact that each of these men died of AIDS may, I realize, cast a pall over the extraordinary union they managed to create, but it also magnifies and makes even more poignant the beauty of that union, which did not fade until the last of the lights in the group went out. In fact, by their best reckoning, each man in the group had already contracted

AIDS by the early 1980s: none was on an obviously self-destructive streak; none went out and sought sexual suicide by having unprotected sex. Each was a product of the seventies; "unprotected sex" had no real meaning when these young men played hard in the sexual arena.

By the time the last one died—he was significantly the "father" of this sexual and emotional family, the one who had brought the group together—I realized I'd witnessed something unique, even awe-inspiring. Charles was the ringleader, a brilliant classics scholar who came from a family broken by divorce after divorce—he had at least three different stepfathers—but who didn't seem to be especially damaged by this shattered experience of a nuclear family. Indeed, it seemed to give him a model for the sexual clan he ended up founding. He met Warren in the early 1970s and they became what I think of as rogue lovers: emotionally devoted to each other, certainly sexually turned on by each other, but sexually voracious, they engaged in any number of threesomes and foursomes, and Warren, especially, haunted the many bathhouses that New York then boasted, happily getting fucked by as many men as he could. Charles and Warren contrasted sharply in personality: Charles was a sort of Dr. Spock, with a photographic memory, a fiercely logical mind, and an encyclopedic grasp of everything from Sophocles to linguistics to Talmudic law. Some found his manner cold and peremptory: he said what he thought and corrected you when he thought you were wrong (which was often). Warren, on the other hand, was entirely mellow: he liked to smoke pot, he tended masses of potted plants and flowers in his exposed-brick East Village apartment, and pretty much smiled through life— he had a disarming sweetness. He was also a talented commercial artist and, while he never dared to one-up Charles, was quietly just as intelligent and in many ways as well-informed. Charles and Warren, through their energetic sexual escapades, eventually attracted Steve, a computer programmer just when computer programmers were first sought after (he made a lot of money), who fell wildly in love with Warren, but eventually accepted Charles's preeminent place in Warren's life and simply made himself available when Warren could hack it. Three more men eventually joined the group: an ex-lover of Charles's, Sean, a high-school English teacher whom Charles decided he still wanted to see now that Warren occasionally spent time with Steve; Sean's lover, Julio, a sweet Venezuelan who spoke little English but seemed to understand everything that went on around him through some sort of psychic gift; and Jaime, an observant Jew with whom Charles and Warren once had a stirring threesome, who was intrigued by the warmth and candor and pleasure of the group.

There's no need to keep all these names in any sort of order—I often couldn't—but the fact that there's no need is part of the point: it almost didn't matter who happened to be with whom on any given day or night. Because he was used to shuttling back and forth from one home to another (a pattern for which his childhood had amply prepared him), Charles had, for a long time, no apartment of his own—he'd just stay with Warren or Sean or Jaime as the moment decreed. It's not that there weren't squabbles or eruptions of jealousy among the six: there were; indeed, they staged some lively soap operas. But after every moment of high drama, the group just seemed to bind closer together: some basic pact held. The unmistakable feeling you had, watching this kaleidoscope of relationships shift and change, was this: these men cared about each other. And they cared about each other in the effortlessly natural way that *family* can care about each other. But the group was richly sexual: perhaps because of the built-in variety of their situation, these men continued to find each other hot. Sometimes one or another temporary satellite would be brought in—Warren continued his private orgies at the

baths and continued to attract this or that additional admirer—
but the basic unit of the group soon coalesced into the six of
them. And it stuck. It stuck for as many years as each of these
men was alive.

When Steve got sick, the rest of the group took care of him,
as simply and unquestioningly as a mother takes care of a sick
child. When Steve died, by which time Warren had become sick,
the remaining members of the group just grew closer. They all
strongly suspected now what their collective and separate ends
would be, but there was a kind of spiritual peace—a feeling of
acceptance that I find difficult to describe, except that you felt it
whenever you were near these men. Sean went next; then Julio;
then Jaime. Warren somehow hung on, and it was hard not to
feel that Charles, who had fathered this whole clan, somehow
psychically, somatically decided not to get sick until Warren
died. It was as if they had made some tacit pact: Charles had to
see Warren out before he could himself leave.

When Warren died, Charles finally succumbed, too: his de-
terioration was rapid, as if he had willed it. My ex-lover was his
final caretaker; Charles knew it was finally time to release his grip
on the reins—nothing if not practical, he made it clear, in his
usual abrupt way, that he needed my ex-lover to take care of him,
something my ex-lover had the strength and heart as a friend to
do. Charles retained his sharp, cold mind to the end; there was
nothing sentimental about him—I don't think I ever saw him cry.
But he had shown, in the immense care, enjoyment, and patience
he had evinced through his actions toward the whole "married"
group he'd engendered, the clearest, deepest, and most abiding
love I think I have ever seen. Reflecting on this extraordinary
group fueled one of my main motives to write this book: I didn't
want what they had achieved to go unremarked. I've changed
their names, but not the truth of the quiet and unquestioned love
they created and experienced among themselves.

I'm not sure what the moral is here—or that there particularly is one. But I have no doubt that my aerial view of the Charles clan has evoked some strong memories of your own of similar groupings—maybe you're part of one right now. If you are, you're lucky. You're experiencing a kind of revolutionary gay marriage, which, as Frank Browning said, has implications and even offers a potential model for all of the rest of us—straight or gay.

Not, of course, that this clan approach is right for everyone. Whether the result of cultural and family indoctrination, or some innate human need to couple, most people, including gay men, when they face the prospect of love seem to yearn for one other lover. It is in these couplings that we confront the most psychological baggage: while it's true that we may not have many gay models of marriage, we do, consciously and unconsciously, cart around the model of our parents' relationship—or the relationships of whatever caretaker(s) brought us up. Not only the union we saw between those parents and caretakers, but the relationship we each had to each of them. This is, of course, the stuff of every couples self-help book, every women's magazine, every talk show on television: how can we stop repeating these unconscious patterns and forge a new, "authentic" union with the partner we've chosen?

This is not a debate in which I especially want to engage. My battle-worn observations, from my own life and from looking at a huge range of gay male couples, tell me that we're never entirely able to escape the models we grew up with: they're stained indelibly into our psyches; we're stuck with them. A good deal of making any marriage work seems to me to require accepting the harsh truth that you're always, in some way, going to get on each other's nerves. As a therapist friend of mine says (and he's been more or less happily monogamous with his lover for the past twelve years), "Other people are a bitch." Quentin Crisp goes further: *"Live alone,"* he instructs us. "The continued propinquity of another person cramps the style after a time unless that person is somebody you think you love. Then the burden becomes intolerable at once." Based on common, weary human experience, this is a defensible stance.

But many of us don't want to live alone. Which means that many of us throw ourselves blindly into the weird mix of coupling, weird because most of what we bring to each other is unconscious—which doesn't generally start to grate until we've begun having a "long-term relationship." Charles repeated a family pattern that worked more than not for his five cospouses, who, for various reasons of their own (probably based on their own family models), found it satisfying. But as wonderful, loving, and in a certain way, marital as it was, the built-in variety helped to sustain it. Had you sequestered Charles and Warren in the same room for longer than a week, they'd have started throwing Warren's potted begonias at each other.

The word *pact* repeatedly occurred to me in describing the Charles clan because that was the bedrock sense you had about what finally kept those guys together: they had somehow, fundamentally, made the decision to stay together. I think the idea of a pact also offers an essential key to any more conventional coupling that works. It has to go deeper than words. Something in the psychic basement has to be shifted and secured for any marriage to sustain itself.

We get back to sex: if there is—as I believe, under the potent and persuasive sway of Camille Paglia, William Allman (in his aforementioned book *The Stone Age Present,* which offers evidence of strong evolutionary roots for the male promiscuous urge), and from my own passionate feelings, observations, and experiences—a strong drive in men to rove sexually, are two gay men always at odds with the idea of a monogamous marriage? How is it possible to square what seems to be this fundamental roving urge with the pact to couple?

I should say that many gay men I've talked to don't agree with me that men are natural sexual rovers. They accuse me of rationalizing my own past urges to stray. But the monogamous couples I have talked with who seem successfully faithful to each other (as opposed to miserably faithful, of whom I can cite more numerous examples) do seem to have created a capacious sexual playground for themselves: they may be the only players in the sandbox, but they have a great time thinking up new games. This doesn't mean (necessarily) that they continually contrive new ways to use whipped cream and clotheslines; but it does mean that they've worked out a way to satisfy their desires in some essential way.

I said before that the idea of compromise seems to me problematic: when you dilute pleasure, especially sexual pleasure, when you attempt to round off its edges to conform with what you perceive to be somebody else's expectations, some infant, raging part of you just gets mad—raging mad. It's that unconscious scream, that insatiable id, again: *I want what I want and I want it now.* All of what we've talked about before applies: Dionysus has a fierce and unredemptive sucking gravity; Apollo will shoot, dammit, in the direction he wants to shoot, no matter what you (or your superego/conscience) want him to do. Frank Browning is eloquent about this unredeemable quality of sexual "ecstasy":

> *The impulse toward the ecstatic speaks of neither good nor evil, neither protection nor redemption. It speaks only to remind us that the permanent human condition is exposure, and it reveals that the new activist demand for sexual "safe space" is little more than a silly oxymoron. On the one hand, "safe space" denies the darkness and violence humans face in nature, and on the other hand it concocts a language of banal, "redemptive" sexual management that would sup-*

press the inherently transgressive nature of desire. (The
Culture of Desire, *p. 104)*

A successful union between gay men (monogamous or not)
has, it seems to me, to provide for each partner's raging id—it
has to take into account the inescapably "transgressive" nature
of sexual desire. There can be, in a sense, no compromise: in some
basic satisfying ways, the "ids" of both gay male spouses must be
served or (from my observations) it's splitsville. Gay men trip
themselves up when they think—or slip back into an unconscious
rut of reacting as if—marriage means being "nice" according to
some (usually heterosexual) model they either knew from their
parents as children or yearned to believe was true (more usually
the latter).

There may be such a thing as compromise about who takes
out the garbage and who loads the dishwasher: this is part of the
grubby, unavoidable reality of any live-in relationship. But sexually, we have to provide for each other in very different ways.
Any possibility of even momentarily joyous monogamy seems to
me impossible if we don't. Of course, our ids rage for more than
sexual satisfaction; we also crave warmth and security and trust.
But even these more conventionally aboveboard desires (desires
we can talk about to our mothers) need to be met in certain specific ways our unconscious minds require.

We've touched (barely) the issue of intimacy as a use of sex:
what we saw in bodybuilder Brad and his lawyer lover Jim was
a shared moment of "exposure," to use Frank Browning's word.
The value wasn't simply in exposing, however: it was learning
from what was exposed something more about what the exposer
needed. It was *seeing* the revealed soul that led to any kind of nur-
turing, satisfying, or lasting intimacy. We saw in Angelo, as he
confessed (crying, knees locked, in the pouring rain) his sheer-
sock fixation to Danny, another example of this difficult, fertile

self-exposure. Danny accepted what was "exposed," then, sensing the urgency of Angelo's need, incorporated it into their sex life. Something was learned, responded to, and fed back: the id got its way.

Sensitizing ourselves to each other's unconscious requirements takes vigilance, and it can be exhausting, both for the confessor and the confessee: we can be forgiven when we regress (as everyone I know in a relationship continually does) to old blind, in-a-rut patterns. You can't live in a state of continual, painful self-exposure: sometimes you gotta take a nap, eat a pizza, or watch Mary Tyler Moore reruns. But some repeated return to opening the soul seems to have to happen for any kind of satisfying union to continue. We have to pay attention to each other. Perhaps, taking our cue from the Charles clan, we also have to make a pact to pay attention to each other.

Paying this kind of intimate attention, especially in the realm of sex, and especially over time with one other person—a "lover"—brings us into deeper and, to me, inescapably "spiritual" realms. When we go down and muck about in the Dionysian underworld with someone else, when we negotiate what sort of Apollo each us is going to be in this "transgressive" realm, we're playing with some pretty hot stuff. This is one of the places love is forged.

"TO MAKE US FEEL EXISTENCE": A PRACTICAL TAKE ON SPIRITUAL SEX

I'm making what may at first seem to be an abrupt and worrying transition: the word *spiritual* generally makes me as instantly suspicious and resistant as I (perhaps erroneously) anticipate it makes you. But, actually, we've been preparing for this descent on the elevator throughout this book.

My take on spirituality, especially as regards sex, doesn't happen somewhere in the ineffable ozone: it happens, is felt, is explored, is enjoyed right here in the muddy earth. Paradoxically, it's in that chthonian muck I've gone on about that we find the roots of what I call spirituality: a sense of connection that somehow transcends both partners in a union to create something larger than either could have conceived on his own. The love that seems to create itself out of this muck is not susceptible to coercion. It blooms in the interstices, sneaks in through the back door. Remember the quality of caring Dirk (with his multiple selves) received from his lover Joe—we were told nothing more than that Joe didn't bolt when he met the frightening "Hank": he stayed and listened and cared. Some capacity psychically to embrace Dirk and his warring selves simply happened in Joe—it was there without either Dirk or Joe forcing or even beckoning to it. The Charles clan grew love like Warren grew flowers and plants: some pact flowered on its own—there is no way that I know of to explain this flowering, no reductive psychoanalytic theory that does justice to the power and immanence of the love these men found, knew, and used.

I know of no more powerful writer about the spiritual content of love than Thomas Moore, whose books, including *Care of the Soul,* deserve to be the best-sellers they are. If I could recommend one reading assignment, it would, in fact, be *Care of the Soul:* it explores the mystery and profound disturbances and joys of the spirit, connecting them with our day-to-day experience in astonishing and—that word again—spiritually satisfying ways. He helps bring focus to our topic right now, as well as offering a perspective that embraces many of the themes we've so far explored, particularly about the "soul's proper yearnings"—analogous to the psyche's impulse to cure itself—and the often oblique, unsettling nature of sex and love:

Love brings consciousness closer to the dream state. In that sense, it may reveal more than it distorts, as a dream reveals—poetically, suggestively, and, admittedly, obscurely. If we were to appreciate truly the Platonic theory of love, we might also learn to see other forms of madness, such as paranoia and addiction, as evidence of the soul's reaching toward proper yearnings. Platonic love is not love without sex. It is love that finds in the body and in human relationship a route toward eternity. In his book on love, Convivium—*his answer to Plato's* Symposium—*Ficino, who is credited with coining the phrase "Platonic love," says concisely, "The soul is partly in eternity and partly in time." Love straddles these two dimensions, opening a way to live in both simultaneously. But incursions of eternity into life are usually unsettling, for they disturb our plans and shake the tranquility we have achieved with earthly reason. (Pp. 82, 83)*

The achievement and experience of love isn't the single-minded thing so many love gurus—Marianne Williamson, Leo Buscaglia, and Louise Hay come to mind—often seem to preach. For example, for Williamson (and "The Course in Miracles" she espouses) there are two basic, opposed forces: love and fear. A potent idea—it has the stun-power of truth. But it doesn't prepare us for, or do justice to, the complicated, internal war of the psyche, which mixes love and fear subtly, obliquely, and manifests the war bafflingly. Love and fear may get to the bone, but the words alone don't help us to understand the skin, fat, muscle, and blood that sheathe the bone and give enigmatic form to the body and self.

Thomas Moore addresses the subtleties of flesh as well as the schematic skeleton, which I maintain we must do, too, to achieve anything approaching satisfying love. We must learn, continually, to tease out the meanings of our fantasies, fears, loves, and hates. This is a sometimes tortuous process. As Moore writes:

> *Textures, places, and personalities are important on the soul path, which feels more like an initiation into the multiplicity of life than a single-minded assault on enlightenment. As the soul makes its unsteady way, delayed by obstacles and distracted by all kinds of charms, aimlessness is not overcome. . . . (p. 259)*

He quotes a portion of Keats's "Endymion" to telling effect; as Moore puts it, "Keats describes this soul path exactly" (p. 260):

> *But this is human life: the war, the deeds,*
> *The disappointment, the anxiety,*
> *Imagination's struggles, far and nigh,*
> *All human; bearing in themselves this good,*
> *That they are still the air, the subtle food,*
> *To make us feel existence.*

Learning to "feel existence" is something Rick, thirty-five, and Chris, twenty-nine, are finally discovering for themselves. The first three of their seven years as lovers were spent mostly apart: Rick was finishing a Ph.D. in economics at a university in another state, and, as Chris puts it, "we waged a love affair on weekends and holidays—some of the most incredible moments we've had. We were just so damned happy to see each other whenever we could. Absence absolutely made the heart grow fonder."

Chris, who works as a buyer in a major department store in Cleveland, Ohio, says it was much tougher going when Rick finished grad school and moved in with him. "Rick hoped to get a good banking job and discovered pretty quickly that the commercial world didn't care a hell of a lot about doctorates in economics. He was really discouraged. He finally ended up, after a grueling year where I supported him and he felt guilty about my supporting him, getting a lower-level manager job at a small suburban Cleveland bank—something far below what he felt he was capable of. The 'real world' clubbed him in the face. I knew he was angry, but he shut down about it. In fact, now that he was living with me, and maybe out of guilt for the financial support I'd given him over that first year, he became incredibly accommodating. Sometimes I'd feel I had some polite cousin living with me—with whom I sneaked sex in the dark. When I visited him at his grad school, he was completely different—competent, funny, irreverent, and sexually adventurous. He'd flip through *The Joy of Gay Sex* and purr at me, 'Why don't we try *this,* hon?' pointing to one or another *Kama Sutra*–type position. But when he moved in with me, it's like that whole adventurous, hopeful self got swatted down, like a puppy who'd been hit once too often with a newspaper. It was heartbreaking to see this kind of 'death' in Rick—but after a year or so, my sympathy started to wear thin. It's not like I want to be a department-store buyer for the rest of my life—I've got higher aspirations, too. My secret desire has been to take courses in interior design and renovation and eventually set up my own consulting firm. I'm trying to stash away enough money to let me scale down to part-time at the store so that I can do that. In the meantime, we have to pay the rent. That's life. I got angrier at Rick the more he shut down. I was younger than he, but sometimes I felt older: why didn't he just grow up? But it was hard to call him on anything. I mean, he wasn't outwardly morose. He kept up this perfectly serene facade—smiling, deferring to me, obviously trying to be who he thought I wanted him to be. But he was disappearing more and more, retreating somewhere deep inside himself where nobody—including me—could get at him.

Like I said, my sympathy soon turned to anger and frustration. I started sniping at him. Inventing reasons to get mad, stupid reasons, like lecturing him on how to load the dishwasher. But he kept on taking it. He was like an emotional punching bag: he'd absorb whatever blows I threw without wincing. And sex—well, maybe it's not surprising, but I started to get more aggressive in bed, to bring my anger into our sex life. I'd slap his ass, hard, repeatedly, something I'd never done before, then fuck him, sometimes without lube, as brutally as I could. It was peculiarly satisfying to me—hitting him, fucking him, almost raping him. It's like I wanted to slap, punch, fuck my way through the barrier he'd put between us. In a way, we had the hottest sex we'd ever had. But the more brutal I got, the more he withdrew later on, after we were done fucking and resumed 'living.' His two main expressions were 'That's nice, hon' or 'I'm sorry, hon.' After a while, I felt I wasn't living with anybody. He was just some shell who did the dishes and took my dick up his ass. That may sound sort of hot in some disembodied pornographic scenario, but it was actually hell."

Chris did something he says he's ashamed of, but which nonetheless led to a breakthrough for both of them. "I decided to go away for the weekend, and not tell Rick. I think what I wanted to do was disappear, physically, completely, with no warning or explanation—maybe to make it clear how much I hated Rick's own inner disappearing act. So, one Friday night, Rick came home and found an empty apartment. I found out later that he freaked. By Saturday morning, he'd even called the police. I'd checked into a Holiday Inn, with a bunch of books and junk food. I felt guilty, but there was some absolutely nasty and delighted imp in me savoring the pain I was sure I'd caused Rick. The sadistic urge to hurt him I'd started to bring into our sex life just took over completely. Let him sweat, I thought to myself. Let him get the kick in the gut he'd been giving me without knowing it. Let him *feel* something."

When Chris returned late Sunday night, he found Rick in a state of near collapse—which turned, quickly, into the fiercest rage he'd ever seen Rick feel or display. "I was really afraid he'd haul off and slug me," Chris said. "He just kept shouting, 'How *dare* you? How *dare* you do this to me?' " Chris positioned himself behind a couch, out of range of his spitting lover's fists, which Rick proceeded to bang against the wall like a madman. "I fucking bend over backwards to please you, you asshole," Rick hissed at Chris, who had never heard Rick use the words *fucking* or *asshole* before. "And you just fucking disappear on me. What the hell did you think you were doing? Don't you realize we're fucking *married*? You don't do this to someone you supposedly *love.*"

Chris didn't speak for a moment. He just looked at the livid Rick. Then he said the first words that came to his mind: "Thank God."

"Thank the fuck *who?*"

"Thank God you're letting me know you *feel* something."

Rick looked baffled. Then, abruptly, he slumped onto the couch Chris was standing behind. His back to Chris, Rick dropped his head onto his chest and covered his face with his hands. He began to cry. He finally whispered, "You don't think I *feel* anything?"

Chris said he walked out from behind the couch and sat down next to Rick. They began to talk with each other, with some of the same relief and release we saw in Brad and Jim after Jim walked in on Brad's pot-saturated beat-off session with the photo of his father. "I thought you *knew* how I felt," Rick said. "I mean, the way we've been having sex—all that aggression— I thought that meant you knew what I wanted from you. Someone to be *forceful* with me. Someone to knock me around. Someone to treat me like the fuck-off I really am." Chris said, "Yeah, maybe down deep somewhere I was getting the message about how hurt and angry you were. But we never *talked* about it. You turned into some Stepford husband. You *left* me—don't you see? That's why I had to leave you."

Chris and Rick realized they had had a surface life and a deep unconscious sexual life—but nothing in between to connect them. "It's not enough," Chris said to Rick, "to just sort of act out anger like we do in bed. It just makes the rest of our life seem like a lie. Everything except sex is so hollow: there's just nothing there most of the time. You know what the problem is? You're *lying* to me. You're not telling me what you want. You're not telling me when you're pissed off. Maybe I want to be manhandled a little, too. Not because I think I'm a fuck-off, but because I want something raw and real from you. Come back to me. *Talk* to me. Be with me. I don't think you know that I can take your hate, even your self-hate. I'm not going to go away. Let it out—please just let it *out.*"

Chris stops a moment as he relates all this to me, then says, shaking his head, "It sounds so banal when I tell you the details. Like *One Life to Live.* But I knew that Rick had never been told it was all right to share the stuff he felt shame about. It's not that he grew up in a tight-ass WASP family: in fact, the problem was pretty different. His family is this great big, sprawling, Italian mess of noisy brothers and sisters—Rick was caught in the middle, thought he had to be the mediator, and learned to keep a passive front very early on. 'There was so much *noise* in my house,' he told me. 'I just wanted to escape.' But he'd escaped too far into himself for anyone to see him. I was fucking him like a wild, angry beast because it was the only way I knew to *bore* into him—all too literally. But I don't want to have that be the only way we connect. I want to bring whatever 'real' person I find when we have sex out into the light. I want our whole life to feel authentic, not just our sex life."

Rick has begun to emerge, Chris tells me. "He needed to

get angry. He needed to connect to the feeling of wanting to kill me before he could connect to loving me. He needed to feel more of who he was, all of who he was. And now, when I bark at him for putting glasses in the wrong way into the dishwasher, he'll sometimes look up at me, in his old sweet way, and say, 'Fuck off. Mind your own business.' " Chris exhales slowly, then says in a quiet but powerful voice, "There's someone *there* now. I've been waiting for so long for Rick to start to *exist*. Now he does."

The authentic part, the spiritual part, of Rick and Chris's relationship had found, even before the blowup and break-through Chris described, some expression in sex: this was, in fact, for a long time, the only arena in which they could manage to "feel existence." But it wasn't enough. Their ids wanted more. A whole marriage comes from people who each feel whole themselves. Fucking, slapping, manhandling, Rick as Chris did was a scream from his soul that he needed, wanted, more self from Rick than he was getting. Sometimes it takes genuine wrath to rip through the thick flannel defenses that smother authenticity, that smother the spirit. Our psyches want it all: sex, certainly; but also a feeling that you're connecting in the rest of life. This means, as Chris told Rick, having the courage to let out your hate as well as your love—to be as much of all of who you are—not just internally, but with somebody else.

TOWARD A FRUITCAKE MODEL OF SELF

Jungians out there must be wringing their hands in frustration. "Don't you know Jung talked better about all this archetypal, anima/animus, dark and light, Hero's Journey model of self, better than anyone? Why aren't you quoting *Carl?*"

A sort of general Jungian perspective has actually saturated this book: Camille Paglia's forces of darkness and light, of the feminine, underworld Shaman and the masculine, cut-abbed Warrior; Freud's warring drives of Eros and Thanatos; Mark Simpson's, Leo Bersani's, and Michel Foucault's concepts of the relativity and masks of gender; Frank Browning's warning that there is no "sexual 'safe space' "; the necessary, spiritual aimlessness of the soul's path we get from Thomas Moore (and Keats); not to mention every slice of sex and emotion offered by each man in this book—all seem to me to have resonance with Jung's archetypal view of the self.

I invoke Jung now not merely to add more substance and color to the illustration of the ambivalent and ambiguous spiritual and sexual components of self we've been drawing all along, but to add an essential note about the achievement of wholeness—of *integrating* those components—we haven't so far heard. Jung sounds it in a letter he wrote in 1958:

> *I cannot possibly tell you what a man who has enjoyed complete self-realization looks like, and what becomes of him. I never have seen one, and if I did see one I could not understand him because I myself would not be completely integrated. . . . I had to help innumerable people to get a bit more conscious about themselves and to consider the fact that they consist of many different components, dark and light.*

"A bit more conscious": is this all we can hope for? The vagueness of the phrase might, depending on our momentary cast of mind, either inspire optimism or pessimism: how much is "a bit"?

I started with the story of my lover and me. I'd like to end with "a bit" more of that story. What it illustrates, I think, isn't only connection, but fallibility; however, through that fallibility, maybe even because of it, it's also a story about the sexual mystery and strangeness of love.

On a recent Saturday night, my lover and I got crazy. We chalked up our urge to do something sexually over-the-top to the endless disgruntlements of each of our workweeks: I felt as if I were drowning in my twenty-six writing and editorial projects; everyone wanted everything done yesterday. My lover was similarly overwhelmed: his clients were snapping at his heels like rabid dogs. We'd had enough of being nice to everybody. We wanted, somehow, to let 'er rip. But how?

The phone lines: you'll remember our ambivalent attachments to those sex providers. What about putting a really outrageous message on one—no, hell, every single one of them—and see whom we could get to call? We had the idea of auditioning tops to help me "work my buddy over." Our sex life can get pretty rough: my lover likes his chest "worked on" (nipples caressed and twisted), some controlled slapping to the face, a little bit of bondage—and the kind of inspired verbal abuse to which I'd discovered, over the months and years of letting go with him, I had endless access. (I didn't realize how rich and infinite my sexual imagination was until my lover helped me to unleash it. It still blows me away, the power of Apollo sucking Dionysus' dick, taking in that dark fluid and flying with it to places he never knew existed.) The thought of inviting one or two other topmen to join us, in ways we hadn't really worked out yet—the fantasy was compelling but a little vague in detail—fed, I think, that urge for sexual variety that I continue to maintain is innate in men—and certainly was turning on my lover and me.

I turned out most of the lights in my little studio, told my lover to get naked and wait for me in bed, stripped down to a version of that Vault jock-strapped beast I've already described—complete with mirror shades, black leather biker jacket, and scuffed black Army boots—felt my voice travel down to my crotch (that gym-teacher pitch lives somewhere in my balls), and proceeded, methodically, to leave five or six of the hottest messages I've ever left in my life, while my lover writhed, getting more and more excited, listening to each one, on my bed. I described us accurately enough—me the tough, bearded sadist in his forties, he the preppy, cute bottom in his thirties—but kept the message somewhat vague to attract the widest audience, but making it clear we liked it "rough."

When I was done, I instructed—I'd now *become* my high school football coach—my lover to get up from the bed, walk over to me in front of the chair I was sitting in, while I stroked his chest—which makes him wild—and told him slowly, step by step, what I was going to do to him that night, and what we were going to have the third or fourth or fifth top do to him. As if on cue, the phone started ringing. We listened as my answering machine logged one testosterone-soaked voice after another. I made various comments about each caller leaving a message on the tape, while I continued to play with my lover's nipples, while he continued to stroke his dick, my raspy voice now completely soaked with sex and danger: "Yeah, he sounds like he might be okay, six-two, two hundred twenty pounds—you like skinheads, boy?" My lover's dick jumped. One voice after another slipped onto the tape: "Yo, sounds hot, I'd like to beat the fuck out of that kid while you hold him up." "Been jerking off to your message. I'm short, muscular, stocky, with a goatee, and love to get rough—can I bring over a buddy?" "You like tough Latinos? Your kid like to get fucked by a ten-inch dick?" "I'm hot, bisexual, I got a girlfriend, so you can't call me back, but I'll try you later. Uh—does your kid mind getting bruised?" The voices piled onto each other as I led my lover back to the bed, where I proceeded to push him down, straddle him, and slap him twice across the face while I continued my nonstop sex talk, punctuated by more and more hungry male voices on the tape clicking off and on, imagining out loud how I could get my lover to service two, three, four, maybe a whole fuckin' roomful of different horny tops, let them each do exactly what they wanted to, subject him to whatever creative torture they felt like inflicting, let them have all the time they needed, while I instructed them about what part of my lover's body needed to be worked on next, when he'd get fucked, when he'd have to suck dick. My slaps were like punctuation marks as I wove a wilder and wilder story of the endless night, morning, weekend sex I was setting up for him—it wouldn't stop until every single one of these men was satisfied in exactly the way he wanted it.

We couldn't hold it. My lover shot his load first (hitting the wall); I jammed myself down onto the bed, holding him, getting off on the smell of our sweat and my black leather jacket, and had one of the most incredible orgasms of my life.

We exhaled from the bottoms of our feet: Apollo and Dionysus collapsed back into their beds, starving for rest.

Unfortunately, those damned topmen didn't know we were through. We underwent that familiar transformation from a state of raging sexual hunger to a state of complete satiation, where the thought of any of the "hot" details we'd just lavished each other with was, not exactly unpalatable, just profoundly off the point. But this distance from our raging sexual selves—my voice had returned to its normal quiet, high baritone; my lover was his cuddly, sleepy little-boy self—allowed us a new vista, a new perspective, about the voices that kept pouring, one after another, onto my tape. It was absolutely fascinating—and poignant and wonderful and frightening. The deluge of *hunger*— my messages had obviously tapped a nerve in a lot of men, and it was as if each one of them ("offering themselves," as Camille Paglia said, "without cost to random strangers") was revealing the most intimate, naked, primal, aspects of himself; we were being given a powerful, if baffling, *gift* from men whose names we would never know: a pure gift from the least blocked regions of self.

"Sometimes," Marguerite Yourcenar writes, in the quote from *Alexis* that began this book, "alone, before a mirror which redoubled my anguish, it would occur to me to ask what I had in common with my body, with its pleasures or its ills, as if I did not belong to it. But I do belong to it, my dear. This body, which appears so fragile, is nonetheless more durable than my virtuous resolutions, perhaps even more durable than my soul."

We belong to our bodies; they are full of a wisdom and spirit that nudges us unceasingly, if mutely—a wisdom expressed in each voice of every turned-on man who left a message on my answering machine. The wisdom is as full of longing and sorrow as hope and desire; it knows mortality and therefore knows the precariousness and preciousness of pleasure. The abrupt transition from sexual beasts to thoughtful human beings my lover and I underwent in the moment after orgasm, somehow this transition, this reentry into "conscious" life, made more remarkable by the sound track of aching men who hadn't yet made this shift, men still in the stink of sexual chthonian darkness—it allowed us to see, clearly, the depth and power of desire, the grace of it, the sureness of it, the rightness of it . . . and the limits of it. It allowed us to see our own limits, too. In our crazy sexed-up state, we'd opened (once again) that Pandora's box of possibility: while we decided we really didn't want to meet with an actual third or fourth or fifth top, when the fantasy returns, it returns with horrific force, and we both once again worry that either I or he will give in to it, privately or together, in ways we'll regret later on. We always have to pull on the sails to redirect the boat—each new foray into the sexual ocean requires alertness, an alertness it's hard to maintain in the roar of a sex fantasy. And there was, of course, the messy reality of our callers: since we weren't actually talking to any of them, I was risking getting repeat pissed-off messages at all hours of the night from frustrated tops. Sex is a potential, sometimes an actual, mess. But it's a mess my lover and I take on, bit by bit, willingly, willing to renew our pact to contain the forces that drive us—while still getting off on them. Messes are normal: that's maybe our greatest consolation.

The mess continued for me, privately, the next morning. One of the tops we hadn't called back finally got me on the phone and let me have it: "Why the fuck didn't you call me back? I'm sick of you guys leaving messages and playing with my head. Either do it or don't do it. Don't fuck around with me, man." I apologized. The tone in my voice, which had first reflexively gone back to gym-teacher mode, softened. "Phone lines are weird," I said on a sudden impulse. "It's like dreamland. You get to say whatever you want to say. Sometimes you don't actually want to go through with it, though, you know?" My now calmer top friend paused a moment, then said, his own voice modulating to thoughtfulness, "Yeah, I know what you mean. But sometimes you just wanna *act*. And last night, man, I was ready." I told my lover about this phone call; it chastened both of us. "What the fuck were we doing?" my lover asked. "Being human," I suggested.

Sexual appetites are unnerving and disturbing, and as much as they can sometimes lead you to astonishing "great dark moments," they can also slam you into some dark dead ends. The only thing you can count on is that the impelling lava will rise again; the choice we have is, over time, in the wake of past experience, how to react to that rise. There are no safe bets; being sexual, being human, often amounts to a crapshoot. My hope is that we can learn to turn it into a more *conscious* crapshoot. My hope is that we question and resist the strangling model of "mental health" that has too long bedeviled us. As I said earlier on, so many American voices of sweet reason (all those talk shows, magazines, radio psychologists, self-help books, not to mention the PC police) explicitly and implicitly teach us to reach for some sort of morally homogeneous, conflict-free, and completely false ideal of self: a Zen-like state of being in which "love" has forever conquered "fear," in which everything and everyone is ordered, consistent, "happy," "nice," and "calm." But this model is closer to death than life—in fact, it's not a bad *definition* of death. It is nothing to strive for. It is something to *flee*.

We are stained and fallible and full of contradictions: the components of our sexual and emotional and mental lives, of our backgrounds, of the effects on us of genetics and hormones and culture, all stud us with fruits and nuts that are, in the end, irreconcilable. They will always have different tastes and textures, some of them delicious, some of them nauseating, some of them hard, some soft. To aspire to grinding this rich "fruitcake" into a gray, homogeneous mass: what is this but to long for death?

My lover and I, and every reader of this book, are assholes and angels, devils and kings, ordinary people and geniuses, graceful and unspeakably clumsy, cruel and compassionate, beautiful and ugly. It is not only through sex that we learn to locate and accept and even exult in this unmixable mess that makes up each of us: every moment of life affords an opportunity to see our "richness" at work. But sex may bring us most reliably because most primally to the fullest appreciation of all of what we are. Gay men, torn by Apollo and Dionysus, are blessed with an instinct for daring, danger, grace, sweat, love, darkness, and light: if only we could celebrate this uncanny mixture instead of fleeing from it or feeling shame about it! We'll never, Jung tells us, integrate the whole chaotic mix into anything approaching perfection, not as long as the unconscious keeps booting us to new places, not as long as we're alive. If only we'd dance (however gracefully or awkwardly) *anyway,* dance around (and fuck and fantasize about and *love* each other on whatever particular slope we find ourselves on of) that volcano! If only we'd trust and then trumpet what we know, if not to the skies, then at least to each other . . .

"This is it, kid: *sing.*"

BIBLIOGRAPHY

Allman, William F. *The Stone Age Present: How Evolution Has Shaped Modern Life—From Sex, Violence, and Language to Emotions, Morals, and Communities*. Simon & Schuster, 1994.

Bataille, Georges. *Story of the Eye*. City Lights Books, 1987 (1928 ed.; trans. Joachim Neugroschel).

Bawer, Bruce. *A Place at the Table: The Gay Individual in American Society*. Poseidon, 1993.

Bersani, Leo. *Homos*. Harvard, 1995.

Bollas, Christopher. *Being a Character: Psychoanalysis and Self Experience*. Hill & Wang, 1992.

Browning, Frank. *The Culture of Desire: Paradox and Perversity in Gay Lives Today*. Crown, 1993.

Califia, Pat. *Public Sex*. Cleis Press, 1994.

Chauncey, George. *Gay New York: Gender, Urban Culture, and the Making of the Gay Male World 1890–1940*. Basic Books, 1994.

Cooper, Dennis. *Frisk*. Grove Weidenfeld, 1991.

Crisp, Quentin. *The Wit and Wisdom of Quentin Crisp*. Edited by Guy Kettelhack. Harper & Row, 1984.

Foucault, Michel. *The Foucault Reader*. Edited by Paul Rabinov. Pantheon, 1984.

Freud, Sigmund. *A General Selection From the Works of Sigmund Freud*. Edited by John Rickman. Anchor, 1989 (orig. pub. 1937).

———. *Sexuality and the Psychology of Love*. Edited by Philip Rieff. Collier/Macmillan, 1963.

Halperin, David M. *Saint-Foucault: Towards a Gay Hagiography*. Oxford, 1995.

Hocquenghem, Guy. *Homosexual Desire*. Duke, 1993 (orig. pub. 1972).

Jung, C. G. *Letters*. Edited by Gerhard Adler with Aniela Jaffe. Translated by R. F. C. Hull. Princeton, 1975.

Lear, Jonathan. *Love and Its Place in Nature: A Philosophical Interpretation of Freudian Psychoanalysis*. Farrar Straus Giroux, 1990.

McDougall, Joyce. *The Many Faces of Eros: A Psychoanalytic Exploration of Human Sexuality*. Free Association Books (London), 1995.

————. *Theaters of the Mind: Illusion and Truth on the Psychoanalytic Stage*. Basic Books, 1985.

Moore, Thomas, *Care of the Soul: A Guide for Cultivating Depth and Sacredness in Everyday Life*. HarperCollins, 1992.

Paglia, Camille. *Sex, Art, and American Culture*. Vintage, 1992.

————. *Sexual Personae: Art and Decadence from Nefertiti to Emily Dickinson*. Yale, 1990.

————. *Vamps and Tramps*. Vintage, 1994.

Pronger, Brian. *The Arena of Masculinity: Sports, Homosexuality and the Meaning of Sex*. St. Martin's, 1990.

Simpson, Mark. *Male Impersonators: Men Performing Masculinity*. Routledge, 1994.

Stambolian, George. *Male Fantasies/Gay Realities*. Sea Horse Press, 1984.

Yourcenar, Marguerite. *Alexis*. Farrar Straus Giroux, 1986 (orig. pub. 1929).

INDEX